JUMBO JACK'S COOKBOOKS
AUDUBON MEDIA CORPORATION
301 BROADWAY • AUDUBON, IA 50025
1-800-798-2635

GHOSTS

OF

DOOR COUNTY, WISCONSIN

by
Geri Rider

Quixote Press
3544 Blakslee St.
Wever, IA 52658

© *1992 by Geri Rider*

* * * * * * * * * *

Although the author has exhaustively researched all sources to ensure the accuracy and completeness of the information contained in this book, she assumes no responsibility for errors, inaccuracies, ommisions, or any inconsistency herein. Any slights of people or organizations are unintentional. Readers should consult an attorney or accountant for specific applications to their individual publishing ventures.

Quixote Press
3544 Blakslee St.
Wever, IA 52658

3

The reader must appreciate the fact that none of these stories have been published before. Some of them could cause embarrassment to living people today. Because of this, some of the stories use fictitious names. In those cases, it should be understood that any similarity between those names and actual persons, living or dead, is purely coincidental.

DEDICATION

To a very special family. You guys were great support during the writing of these stories. Sorry about the skimpy meals and dirty clothes! A special thank-you goes to all the interesting people who shared their ghost stories.

TABLE OF CONTENTS

FOREWORD

Geri Rider's intimate knowledge of Door County, Wisconsin, serves her well in these accounts of those who join us from another time. . . . .

Whether she speaks of the beaches of Horseshoe Bay or the S-Curve of Georgia Street in Sturgeon Bay, she brings these stories of ghosts to us.

She brings these to us as if we were sitting around the store in one of Door County's general stores.

Professor Phil Hey
Briar Cliff College
Sioux City, Iowa

PREFACE

These are stories of ghosts that have haunted the homes, inns, ships, and woods of our beautiful Door County. Sometimes these stories serve to provide answers to some of the puzzling questions that have long been part of our little corner of the world. Other times they seem to raise new ones.

The Editor

CHAPTER I

THE GUIDE

oor County in the wintertime is entirely different than the warm welcoming Door County of bright summer sun glinting on green fields and blue water. Year-round residents smilingly claim that it's not all that bad 'up here in the winter.' Then they point out that the lake effect of having water on all sides moderates winter temperatures. Of course, they don't mention the fact that all that surrounding water also seems to generate an unusual amount of snowfall which, when whipped about by a three or four-day nor'easter can pile drifts higher than the eaves of a house.

After three weeks of seeing nothing but white dotted by an occasional cardinal searching for seeds a person can get a bit edgy for a change. If this is true on the main peninsula, it's doubly so out on the island.

It was just such a winter that Judd and Hermie got into trouble out on the ice and except for the hand of fate in the shape of a tiny bird the two very well might have perished.

The last weeks of January were bitterly cold with daily snowfall. Only a narrow strip of water remained open between Washington Island and the Northport pier. The ferry schedule was cut back to the bare minimum. There hadn't been any new faces around for weeks. Hermie had a bad case of cabin fever.

Freida always had plenty of little odd jobs lined up at home for Hermie but he far preferred sharing a beer with the boys to listening to his wife

chatter about what birds were at the feeder that morning. Heck, what she wasted on corn in a week would have bought another round of drinks for everybody Saturday night.

When Judd suggested that he and Hermie drive over to the mainland, Hermie didn't think twice before agreeing to the trip. "What about Freida; do you want to take her, too, Hermie?" Judd questioned. Now Judd was a confirmed bachelor, but he considered it only good manners to offer to take his best friend's wife along. That's not to say that he really wanted her to come, however.

"I think not," Hermie answered in his Norwegian lilt. "She'd not be wanting to go to the same places

as us. I'll just bring her back that material she's been wanting for new kit- chen curtains. I've not lived with that woman for better'n thirty years not to know to get around her sharp tongue occasionally." With that deci- sion settled, the two set out in the weak morning sunlight to follow the track across the ice to Ellison Bay.

The gales force winds of a three-day blow had died down overnight leaving man-high drifts in some places. Watery sunlight lent a shiny gleam to the piled snow. Low clouds hung out over the bay looking like a low mountain range, but they were well off to the west and wouldn't roll in until late afternoon.

As usual, a group of men had gotten together just after the first of the year to cut white cedars and dig holes in the ice to set the poles into thus mark- ing a safe car track from the island to the mainland across the ice.

Judd pulled his aged car out onto the ice at Detroit Harbor, and the two cronies sang their way through their favorite drinking songs as they followed the track on it's westward arc well away from the treacherous, undependable ice of the Door.

Out by the passage, a man could be on safe ice one second and adrift on a loose floe or, even worse, plunged into the freezing water the next. Unpredictable winds and currents created ice conditions that not even a fool would knowingly venture onto. Judd and Hermie might have been accused of avoiding a hard day's work whenever possible, but they'd never been labeled fools.

The two thoroughly enjoyed their day of freedom. They drank and talked their way through lunch, remembered to pick up Judd's nails for mending the manger in his barn, and even stopped by the Ellison Bay store to buy curtain material to sweeten Freida's temper.

As they were leaving the store to head home, an old friend stopped to talk and invited them to have a drink with him. Of course, not wanting to seem unfriendly, Judd and Hermie agreed. One drink turned into two; and by the time they pulled the black car back out onto the ice at Ellison Bay, dusk was falling and along with it a light snow.

With the optimism born of perhaps one too many beers, they headed across the ice following the line of trees toward the island. Soon dusk became dark and lightly falling snow became swirling eddies that the headlights of the car couldn't pierce. With a jarring thud, the old car buried itself in a drift. The two men climbed out and attempted to free the car but could push it neither forward nor backward.

Through a break in the storm, Judd swore he saw the lights of Washington Island and the two, their judgment still tempered by Dutch courage, decided to trek home on foot. It was only a few minutes before they lost sight of the car and the line of trees that would have guided them to safety. All around them stinging white snow drifted wildly completely confusing all sense of direction.

"Judd," Hermie's voice was not only cold but also cold sober as the seriousness of their danger struck him. "We're lost and I can't see three foot in front of me. We could be walking straight out into the Door and Clem said there's thin ice a half mile wide and open water in the channel."

"We can't just stay here, Hermie. We'd freeze in a couple of hours. The temperature may be twenty degrees, but that wind feels like it's ten below and getting colder every minute. Faced with the prospect of just giving up or making an attempt to reach safety, the two set out shoulder to shoulder staying within arms reach of each other so that they wouldn't be separated by the blinding snow.

"Judd, do you see a bird?" Hermie's voice was tentative. He was seriously questioning whether or not he was hallucinating. The two had stopped to rest and consider which direction they should be walking. Hermie faced one direction while Judd was turned another.

"I don't see any bird. Nothing would be out on a night like this."

"Not that way. Look over there. Can't you see it? It's right there about waist high." Hermie tugged his friend around facing him toward the tiny bird.

Judd admitted, "Looks like a wren to me. Ain't no wrens around now. They're summer birds. Your wife puts up those houses for them. It can't be there. You're seeing things."

"If I'm seeing things, you are too," was Hermie's logical reply. By unspoken consent, the two set off following the tiny bird. It fluttered just ahead of them, out of reach yet still visible if they watched carefully.

Several times it faded out of sight and they were forced to stop. "I can't see it. Where'd it go?"

Hermie questioned. By now following the tiny bird had become a compulsion with the two.

"There it is over that way." The tiny wren seemed to almost be leading the two men. If they veered off the path, it vanished until they turned the right direction and then fluttered ahead of them as though it were a clear summer day with only the gentlest of breezes.

They trudged through the drifts and blowing snow for what seemed like hours faithfully following a tiny bird that couldn't possibly be there. "Judd, Judd, I see lights! It's the Johannson place at Detroit Harbor. We're going to make it."

"Where's the bird? The bird disappeared," Judd seemed more worried about the little wren's disappearance than about the fact that they were safe. He turned in a complete circle but could find no sign of the tiny bird that had led them through a blinding storm to safety. Without it, they would have surely frozen or fallen through the ice.

The two were welcomed at the Johannson place and thawed out in front of the wood stove as they told their story to the unbelieving family. Neither seemed in need of medical treatment so they were offered rides to their homes.

"See you tomorrow?" Judd questioned his friend.

"No, I don't think so." Hermie answered. "Freida's been after me to repaint her old wren house and build a new one for next summer. I'll be working on that all day."

"You'll not be complaining about her putting bread out for the birds either now, will you?" Judd added knowingly.

"No, that I'll not be doing either," Hermie admitted.

CHAPTER II

THE GLOWING EYES

young boy, his loose-fitting dungarees rolled up to his knees, stops to tighten his suspenders. Wading the Horseshoe Bay beach looking for bits of treasure, broken brightly colored glass or shells washed in by last night's storm, turns into an impromptu swim when a big wave catches him. Now his pants are wet and heavy, dragging at his suspenders.

Being a young boy, he's oblivious to the beauty of the long white beach and blue sky. His bare feet squish in the muddy track, and he kicks the top off a rut left by Ole Anderson's wagon.

A 1967 Chevy, its polished white over blue paint-work gleaming in the bright moonlight, roars down County G south of Egg Harbor slowing for the intersection of County B at Horseshoe Bay. An enthusiastic rendition of the school fight song echoes from its interior. Four girls dressed in matching letter sweaters and pleated skirts sing and chatter gaily.

 What do a boy trudging home in the early 1920's after an afternoon's play and a carload of girls traveling the same area forty some years later have in common?

Young Sven had dallied longer than he should have. He'd been sent to town to deliver Mrs. Nelson's mending for Ma, but then there'd been several games of marbles with his pals on the dirt in front of the abandoned general store. Henry Weborg's best shooter jiggled in Sven's pocket. Henry was hard to beat and Sven aimed to enjoy that shooter until Henry won it back.

His other pocket held his pocketknife and three pieces of polished green glass washed in by the storm along with a couple of fish hooks and a pinch of tobacco sneaked from Grandpa's snuff can. He hadn't had enough nerve to try it yet, but that possession alone made him the envy of his friends.

Right now Sven's main worry was getting home. It's behind the woodshed for him if his chores weren't done before Pa came in from the field, and there wouldn't be any supper until the chickens were fed and Ma's stove wood was carried in.

As Sven came out of the trees along the beach, he saw a tall figure standing at the edge of the dirt road. The boy stopped dead in his tracks. He stood facing an Indian wearing a feathered headdress and carrying a hatchet. The Indian's eyes glowed red as fire.

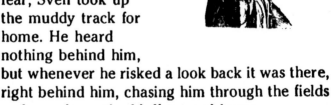

With a whoop of fear, Sven took up the muddy track for home. He heard nothing behind him, but whenever he risked a look back it was there, right behind him, chasing him through the fields and woods up the bluff toward home.

With fear licking at his heels, Sven cinched up his water-soaked trousers with both hands and raced for home heedless of sharp rocks beneath his feet and brambles tearing at his legs.

For weeks, Sven wouldn't walk the path to Horseshoe Bay alone. He never saw the Indian again, and eventually his experience became just a family story retold over Sunday dinner about how Grandpa got scared as a boy.

Perhaps that carload of cheerleaders wouldn't have been so surprised or frightened if they'd known of Sven's experiences, but then again it might have made things worse.

The girls were going to a school sports night when one of them spotted the figure of an Indian in the corner of Horseshoe Bay Park where the carved wooden statue of Chief Oshkosh stood before it was stolen. The figure moved through the trees toward them. When it turned to face the car, the girls saw the glowing red eyes described so many years earlier by Sven.

The Chevy left rubber tracks on the paving as it raced away. None of the girls had any desire to investigate the strange apparition. In fact, they were so shaken by the experience that they missed the sports banquet.

Did Sven and the teenagers see the ghost of a Menominee chieftain or perhaps a fierce Iroquois warrior that terrorized the more peaceful tribes during the early days of the peninsula? How many years will pass before the next unlucky soul will encounter the red-eyed Indian?

CHAPTER III

THE UNWELCOME PASSENGER

t seems that sometimes animals are more sensitive to the presence of unseen spirits than people. At least that appears to be true in this tale.

Over the years, the name of the actual shopkeeper involved in this incident and even the exact year it occurred have been lost in the telling. Since horses and wagons are involved, we'll assume it was either in the late eighteen hundreds or the early nineteen hundreds, probably the latter.

Ephraim had grown from the first tiny cluster of Moravian homes to a fair-sized settlement. Cabins and modest homes clung to the hillside and the flatter land alike. Several enterprising merchants had opened their doors for business, and mostly-passable roads connected the little hamlets that dotted the Peninsula.

Now although Ephraim was considered a religious

town, what with the lack of taverns and all, it still didn't follow that all of the citizens were the most conscientious when it came to their worship habits. One storekeeper in particular whom we'll call Elmer Hanson was remiss in attending services. Elmer's wife would be at church every week with the young ones neatly scrubbed and sitting quietly in a row, but Elmer himself rarely accompanied them. Sunday was Elmer's day for fishing and contemplating how quiet his life was before all the little Hansons came.

Perhaps it was just a continuing string in Elmer's bad luck that it was the parson's buggy that crested the rise just north of Ephraim the day old Jack balked and firmly refused to lift even one hoof off the dusty roadway. Elmer had alternated coaxing and the liberal use of the whip to get the errant animal moving.

Nothing worked. Elmer had just cut loose with a loud string of expletives that would have amazed even a rugged sailor when he was enveloped in the dust cloud raised by a passing buggy.

Even Elmer had the grace to be embarrassed when the Reverend's mellow voice greeted him saying, "Good-day, Mr. Hanson. It appears you're having a spot of trouble with your horse and wagon."

(26)

In a gruff voice, Elmer answered, "The . . ." for a moment he paused awkwardly when he realized the terms he'd intended to use in referring to the horse weren't acceptable in present company. "Yes, Ol' Jack here won't move," he finally replied stiffly.

The parson observed, "It's level ground and your wagon doesn't appear to be heavy loaded. Did something run out and spook him?"

"A rabbit ran between his legs, but that was a mile or so back and rabbits ain't never bothered him before. He's traveled this road hundreds of times."

"Aye," the parson agreed. "He's always appeared a well-broke animal, not skittish or easily spooked."

"He's not been one to ever balk either, and I've had him for nigh onto five years now."

The parson got down from his buggy and stood

at Ol' Jack's head. He took off his hat and scratched his thinning hair before walking around the horse looking at it carefully. He then walked back along the horse's flank to look at the wagon it pulled. Walking up to Elmer he placed his hat on the crown of his head and said, "Mr. Hanson, I do believe I know what your horse's problem is."

Elmer Hanson didn't think any preacher could know more about horses that he did, but by now he was willing to listen to any suggestion. He had a half day's work to do yet and the sun was hanging lower in the sky every minute.

"I do believe that it's the extra passenger in your wagon that the animal objects to."

It was Elmer's turn to scratch his head and examine the loaded wagon. "I don't see nobody in there," Elmer said beginning to doubt the parson's eyesight and perhaps his sanity.

 "There in the back on the keg," the parson pointed. "Tis Lucifer, the devil himself, sitting there. Horses are sensitive to that sort of thing. Your animal will not move til he's gone."

Elmer didn't have as much experience with such matters as the parson, and he hesitated to question the good man's word so he approached the problem from the practical standpoint. "How do we get rid of him so I can get on with my work?"

The parson wasn't above using a little coercion to forward his cause when working with a less than cooperative parishioner and saw his chance to realize the redemption of Elmer and cause him to mend his ways. "Well, Brother Hanson, I couldn't do this for just anybody, but since it's you, one of my loyal flock, I do believe I can help you. It'll be such a personal joy when I look out at the congregation every Sunday to see you there and know that I was able to lend a hand."

Elmer didn't get to be a successful tradesman by being dim-witted. He understood exactly what the person was saying. "Ah, yes, Reverend, it'll be a joy for me, too, hearing your words on Sunday morning."

"Every Sunday morning, Brother Hanson?" the parson asked.

"Why, of course, I meant every Sunday morning," Elmer replied giving credit to the wily preacher. Elmer prided himself on keeping his word when given and the Reverend knew it.

The parson stepped back to his buggy and lifted his dog-eared Bible off the seat.

Then going to the back of Elmer's wagon he opened the book and said a few words before returning to there Elmer stood and said, "I believe your horse will go now, Mr. Hanson."

Elmer still had his doubts, but he climbed up on the seat, picked up the reins, flapped them on Ol'

Jack's back and clucked giddyup to the animal. Jack stepped out into a neat trot.

Elmer was at services that next Sunday and giving him credit, he really did try to keep his word. He worshiped pretty regularly for a couple of months, but then the lure of a quiet morning's fishing found him back with pole in hand Sunday morning more often than not.

CHAPTER IV

THE VANISHING SHIP

 onsidering the vast number of ship wrecks in the Door Passageway, it would be amazing if there weren't some unusual tales involving that treacherous area of water between Washington Island and the northern tip of the Peninsula.

It was an overcast night in late July. An old moon, hung low in the sky, lending a yellow glow to the wispy clouds surrounding it. The Kelly, a small cruiser, was coming through the Door from the east headed for Gill's Rock to tie up for the night when her crew saw a sight they'll never forget.

The two couples constituting that crew had spent the day in Rowley's Bay exploring the Mink River and Newport State Park and had left in the late afternoon, planning to reach Gill's Rock before dark. However, The protected waters of Rowley's Bay had given no indication of just how rough the open water of Lake Michigan had become during the afternoon.

When they left the protection of Rowley's Bay, they were faced with rolling three and four foot

waves and a gale force wind that took their breaths away and strained the small boat's motor. The trip to Gill's Rock would take much longer than the morning trip over. The sun dropped below the tree line of Newport State Park, and dusk settled over the small boat.

After rounding Spider Island, they ran north along shore. The Peninsula offered some protection until they passed Gravel Island and crossed Europe Bay, but when they headed out around the North Port dock into open water, the small cruiser was buffeted by a strong northwest wind that whipped the waves into white caps. The cross currents in the

Door waters made steering even more difficult. It was all the motor could do to push the craft through the rough water.

Dusk had fallen making the Peninsula a dark, hulking shape to their left. A lone gull flew overhead, its wings flapping wildly as it too struggled to make headway in the strong winds.

The outline of Pilot Island and beyond that Detroit Island could be seen when they crested a wave. "Look, there's a light!" yelled one of the women over the howl of the wind.

"It's a ship. I can see lights on the ends and along the sides. It's huge," called her husband. They all peered through the night trying to catch a good look at the boat vaguely outlined in the gloom.

"Is it the ferry headed for Washington Island?" questioned one of the women. "How late is it? Would they still be running?"

As they crested the next wave, the ship passed just beneath

the moon. Three masts, full sails billowing, were silhouetted against the yellow half circle of the moon. The boat itself, a wooden sailing ship of the type used in the Great Lakes in the 1800's, was lit by the golden glow of the moon overhead. It cut through the rough water of the Door headed south, toward Gill's Rock.

The small cruiser dipped into the trough of a wave. When it crested the top of the next wave, the ship had vanished. The small boat crossed where the tall-masted sailing ship had ridden in the waves just moments before, but it was gone as though it had never been.

CHAPTER V

THE GHOSTLY FIGURE

t was long past dusk but not yet midnight. October winds sent brittle leaves across Hill Road. Miniature dancers caught in the uncertain beam of dimmed lights pirouetted for a moment in the spotlight then drifted into oblivion in the surrounding blackness.

Thick fog hung in the air giving a feeling of unreality to every form. Wisps of white nothingness swirled through the dark night changing the shape of each tree, each bush along the paved road until the very landscape seemed to be moving.

The road was familiar. The young couple traveled it hundreds of times a year. The husband sometimes joked that the rusty old blue '65 Chevy could probably make the trip to Sister Bay on its own.

The fog lowered visibility to almost zero making

it a slow trip across the peninsula to Highway 42. The two boys were quiet in the back seat. It wasn't smart to pick a fight with your brother or horse around when Dad was concentrating this hard on his driving.

As they neared the intersection of Hill Road and Old Stage, Karl eased his foot off the gas in anticipation of the upcoming stop sign. On the passenger's side of the car the east drive of the Moravian church on the corner slid past.

Joann was humming along with the Beatles on the softly playing car radio, but the next note caught in her throat, and with a strangled gasp she quit singing.

Karl's surprised voice cut through the sudden stillness, "What the . . . ?" So great was his surprise that the words were left hanging.

A tall man well over six feet in height was walking along the road on the north side of the car. Fog-draped tombstones in the cemetery just behind him created an eerie backdrop.

The man didn't turn at the sound of the approaching car or make any sign that he was aware of their presence. As the car neared the stop sign, he was caught fully in the glow of the headlights giving both the adults in the front seat and the boys in the back a clear view of his appearance.

The figure wore a long topcoat reminiscent of those in style during the years around the Civil War. Perhaps it was the stovepipe hat, the type so often seen in pictures of Abraham Lincoln, that brought up images of that era.

His hands were tucked into the pockets of the dark coat, but all four later agreed that the sleeves hung limply from the figure's shoulders as though his arms were either missing or severely emaciated.

As the car drew up beside the man, the family gasped in unison as they got a good view of the figure. It was the youngest of the boys that put all their thoughts into words. "He don't have no feet. He's floating, not walking."

Indeed, on closer inspection the figure was drifting along the grass. No feet were visible beneath the coat.

The car slid past the man, and Joann and both boys

spun around in their seats to stare at the figure. Once again it was the youngest boy, usually the quietest, that spoke. "He don't have a face neither."

Without the lights of the car to illuminate him the figure was soon swallowed by the drifting fog. If they had turned around and gone back, would the strange apparition still have been there? Did the nearby cemetery have any meaning in the appearance of the ghostly man? Where they the only ones to see the strange figure? Karl and Joann don't think so.

When they told Joann's folks who lived nearby about their strange experience, the father, a rather crusty old farmer, turned to his wife and said, "See, Bea, I told you, but you wouldn't listen."

Unfortunately he thought better of his rash statement and refused to say one word more. He's gone now so we'll never know just what it was he started to say, but even now over fifteen years since they last saw it Joann and Karl peer intently at the grassy road bank along the edge of the cemetery if they're passing that way on a dark, foggy night.

CHAPTER VI

THE GUARDIAN

ince the dawn of time, teenagers have undoubtedly been sneaking away from their parents' watchful eyes to get together with their friends. The maze of lanes and winding back roads that make up Door County's road system are a virtual heaven - sent gift to today's driving youngsters looking for a private hideaway.

The area around Bailey's Harbor with its countless small bays and lanes leading into the timber has long been a favorite partying spot of county teens. One particular area is only accessible by motorcycle, foot, or boat.

The old logging road that provided access to Della Galt's property is rough and overgrown with saplings. During the day a hike down the long lane is a delight. Birds sing in the tall trees that hang over the road, thimble berries and tiny wild flowers bloom and fruit beneath their spreading branches, and you feel peacefully isolated from all the cares and the hurry-up pace of the modern world.

Della's old, two-story guest house sits in a tree-shaded clearing surrounded by innumerable ramsackle outbuildings and tiny cabins. You feel like  you've stepped back into the 1920's. No electric lines lead to the buildings, a hand pump stands by the door, the privy is out back, and the outside cooking and eating area testifies to the practicality of not overheating the main house with summer cooking chores.

Even before her death, Della Galt had quite a reputation. She was respected and liked by the summer visitors that ventured to her quiet Door County haven away from the bustle of early 1900's Chicago and Milwaukee. Della's secluded acreage was one of the first guest houses in the county, and the fact that the proprietor was a bit unusual didn't bother her summer guests.

Della was a small woman with snow-white hair coiled into a tight bun at her nape. Beneath that tiny frame lay a will of iron. She made a success of her guest house when doubters said it couldn't be done, wore men's pants because they were more comfortable, and was a dedicated naturalist before the word had meaning.

Bird feeders stood outside Della's windows. A circle of ground behind the main house was worn smooth by the hooves of deer as they fed at the pans Della filled with corn. The squirrels and raccoons ate from Della's hand and allowed her to pet them. A measure of grain on the beach insured that ducks always floated contentedly in the marshy bay.

It was Della's way with the animals that earned her the reputation of being a witch. Young children claimed that she bewitched the animals and could talk to them and make them do what she wanted.

Della didn't allow hunting on her property, and her sharp tongue fell on the head of anybody who needlessly destroyed any of the wildflowers and other plant life in her woods.

It was Della's dearest wish that her property would be preserved as a natural sanctuary for plants and animals. She hoped that her guest house would be used by nature lovers for many long years after she was gone.

The buildings are now in disrepair and few venture down the old logging road, but some say that although it's been many years since her death, Della still protects the plants and animals in her small domain from careless damage.

The guest house closed shortly after Della's death, and it wasn't long before the track was overgrown. Door County teens soon discovered its isolation and privacy.

The teens tell different stories about Della's place. Some claim that they've heard Della call the animals in to eat and have then seen deer and squirrels gather at the back door of the old house in the moonlight.

A group of older boys were indulging in a drinking party one night and a carelessly tossed can broke a window in one of the cabins. Shortly afterward a wispy figure was spotted in the trees moaning, "Go." The boys scattered in panic leaving their trash behind.

The next afternoon a couple of the boys returned to the cabin. Glass lay on the ground beneath the broken window, but not one of their carelessly discarded cans could be found.

It wasn't long before the teens curiosity led them to explore the old house. An unlocked window was pried up and they gained access to the roomy, old place. To their credit, they have not vandalized the house.

On rainy or cold nights the teens sometimes take shelter inside. They have discovered one very odd characteristic of the old guest house. Even on a still night, a candle will not stay lit in its interior.

Wishing to save their flashlight batteries or perhaps to set a more romantic scene, some of the teens have brought in candles.  Within a few minutes of lighting, the candle will flicker and then a soft breeze will be felt on the faces of those nearby and the flame will be snuffed out as though some one blew on it. The teens swear that Della blows the candles out to protect her treasured guest house from fire.

CHAPTER VII

YOU CAN TAKE IT WITH YOU

 ome called Leonard stingy. Others, more kindly in overlooking his eccentricities, labeled him merely prudent. All were amazed at his evident ability to carry his miserliness to the grave.

Leonard's story dates to the years around the turn of the twentieth century. The only son in a poor immigrant family, Leonard worked from the time he was strong enough to swing an ax and hold up one end of a crosscut saw.

Hours spent alongside his pa cutting cord wood left no time for schooling and little time for play. Leonard's much-mended shirts and cotton pants hung loosely on a frame made spare by little food and long hours of toil.

His sisters married and moved away, but Leonard remained in the small cabin with his widowed mother. After his mother's death, Leonard stayed on in the same aging house patching holes in the roof and shoring up the sagging walls with whatever materials could be had for the taking.

Leonard prided himself on making do. Of course, the pile of scrap wood, rusted tin, and abandoned tools behind his cabin insured that something was certainly always available.

Leonard was known to brag that he kept a dry roof over his head and the cold winter winds out without spending a penny. His neighbors were prone to gaze on his dilapidated home with knowing looks and a shake of the head.

Leonard traded for an almost seaworthy pond net boat and found himself, after considerable patching of the battered hull and torn sail, in the fishing business. Some said that the boat with its leaky hull and oddly patched sail would be the end of its proud new owner, but they were wrong. Leonard met his end fishing the lake but not because of his boat.

In the winter, when the boats couldn't be used because of the ice, the men cut holes in the ice and fished that way. Some even towed sheds out on the lake and lived in them through the week returning home at week's end with their catch to see their families and stock up on supplies for the next week's fishing.

Sail boats, sleds with a sail mounted on them, provided transportation and also a source of competition between the men. The narrow sled frames with their polished runners and billowing sails skimmed neatly over the ice providing fast and efficient winter transport.

Of course, more than one man or boy when testing his prowess on the sail boats ran into trouble. The ice boats had no braking system. If caught in a strong enough wind and unable to turn out of it, the unlucky rider might find himself headed directly for open water. Faced with the alternative of rolling off the speeding sled or taking a dunking in freezing cold water, most risked the loss of their ice boat rather than the loss of their life.

Leonard, however, was not like most men. The one time he got into trouble with his ice boat he refused to roll off to safety and only the hand of fate in a gust of cross wind kept him from being dunked in the icy water. Leonard's sled, although not as fast as most of the other ice boats, was as precious to him as all of his other hard-earned possessions.

When the men set out for the fishing grounds on clear winter mornings, there was always rivalry to see who would get to the fishing spot first. The two or three with the fastest sleds raced ahead with sails billowed leaving the rest of the group to follow at their best pace. At the end of the line would be Leonard's patched sail.

Leonard met his end one February. The month had been warm and some melting had occurred, but the ice was still considered safe. The men sailed

north out of Sister Bay with three or four sleds joining them as they passed the smaller bays. By the time they reached the place they'd been fishing all week, the group numbered eleven men. They opened up the holes they'd been using and dropped their hooks into the freezing water.

As noon approached, the sky clouded over and a strong wind blew up. The men were huddled together eating their lunches when a deafening crack split the air. Every man instantly knew what was happening, but even the most nimble was unwilling to risk jumping the ever-widening ominous black strip of freezing water that divided the ice chunk they sat on from shore and safety.

They were helpless to do anything except watch as the floe they stood on was blown out into open water farther and farther from the solid ice that connected to shore.

The wind whipped the waves into rolling breakers that broke the edges off the floe until all that remained beneath them was a small chunk of ice that tossed wildly up and down ramming into other icebergs until the men were certain that they would either fall off or be crushed. When their's crashed into a much larger chunk, every man quickly scrambled onto it.

All through that long afternoon they huddled together on that piece of ice in the midst of rolling, tossing waves and blinding snow. Not one among them held out much hope of ever returning safely to his home and family.

Their only chance lay in being washed ashore on one of the small islands. With the darkening sky and blowing snow, it was impossible to tell even what direction they were being blown. Not even the most optimistic expected to survive the night.

Miraculously, toward dusk their floe was pushed onto a pile of frozen ice that had formed a temporary island in the lake. Much speculation ensued about where a shoals existed to form the basis for the ice island.

With firmer footing beneath them the men divided what little food was left from their lunches. When mention was made of sharing the food, Leonard drifted away from the group.

One of the more cynical fishermen suggested that Leonard had no intention of sharing anything of his including his last meal with another. Whatever the reason, Leonard settled for the night slightly apart from the rest of the group.

The frozen slabs of ice offered a little wind protection, and the men huddled together through the endless night.

With dawn came the realization that the wind had changed and was blowing in the opposite direction, toward shore. If they were lucky enough to jump on a passing iceberg, they might float back to shore. The risk was great, but staying where they were meant sure death.

Just as they made this decision, one of the men noticed that Leonard was missing. They quickly searched the small ice island but found no sign of Leonard. They assumed he fell into the water during the night and perished.

Less than an hour later a thick slab of ice big enough to carry the remaining ten men rubbed up against the icy island. The men quickly scrambled onto it and then watched as they were blown away from the temporary safety offered by the frozen slabs of ice.

Within a few hours the keenest-eyed young man spotted the bluffs of shore. Even the most pessimistic began to hope that they might reach safety. Before another hour elapsed, they were able to jump to solid ice.

Being no longer at the mercy of the tempermamental lake gave them new energy. They decided to hike back to their fishing spot and retrieve their boats. After an hours' tiresome walking, they sighted the camp.

The men packed their equipment and loaded the ice boats. Their joy at being safe was tempered by the death of Leonard. No matter how odd he might have been Leonard was still one of them and they felt his loss. Somebody pointed out that they ought to take Leonard's things home, too.

When they turned to where Leonard had fished and then to where his ice boat had sat, they saw nothing but frozen ice and their own things.

Leonard's rag tag assortment of fishing gear was gone, and his dilapidated sled with its patched sail was missing, also.

Perplexed by this strange turn of events, they searched thoroughly but found no sign of any of Leonard's things. When one young man ventured to say, "Looks to me like old Leonard managed to take it to the grave with him," he was reprimanded for speaking frivolously of the dead, but the other nine were inclined to silently agree that if anyone could indeed take it with them it would be miserly Leonard.

CHAPTER VIII

THE STONE FIELD GHOST

Y ou boys camping out tonight?"

"Yeah, Dad. There've been a lot of deer tracks around the stone field pond the last few weeks. We thought may be that doe you saw with the twin fawns would come down to drink at dawn and we could get a look at them," Brian answered.

"Be careful if you build a fire back there. It's been mighty dry. It wouldn't take much to light that whole timber," the boys' father admonished before returning to his Advocate.

Brian and Jim loaded their packs and hiked across the farm to the piece of ground dubbed the stone field. It was used for grazing, being far too rocky for farm equipment to go through.

The boys chose a campsite on a small rise some

distance from the pond so they could watch the deer without being so close that the timid animals wouldn't come up to drink.

It didn't take them long to set up their tent and gather wood for a fire. Soon hamburgers sizzled in their iron camping skillet while the boys munched on chips and their sister's chocolate chip cookies.

They listened to tapes and talked until long past dark. Jim flipped off the tape player, and they began competing to see who could identify the most star constellations.

"Jim, look, over there! What's that?" Brian pointed across the open field.

A white light with a wavering, indistinct shape glowed in the middle of the field some distance from their campsite. It hovered slightly above the ground and floated across the field in their direction.

Two equally scared boys began racing across the field toward home and away from the glowing figure. After the first five hundred yards, the rough, rocky ground made treacherous by the darkness and their sore sides caused the boys to slow to a fast walk. At the slower pace, the boys could talk.

"It had to be Dad," Brian insisted. "You know how he likes to scare us."

Jim nodded in agreement, "Come on; if we cut through the timber, we'll beat him back to the house and catch him coming in."

When the boys reached the farmyard, they broke into a run. "Dad's pickup still has the tire off so he had to walk back to the stone field to scare us. There's no way he could have beat us back here," Brian said as the two dashed up the back steps and into the house.

The burst into the kitchen congratulating themselves on catching their dad in one of his pranks. "Hey, the TV's still on."

The two walked into the living room where their dad sprawled in his recliner. In the heat he'd stripped down to his boxer shorts and while the talk show host cracked jokes with his guest their dad lay sound asleep making the little snoring whistle that he made when he fell asleep in his chair and missed the late night news and weather.

The noise the boys made coming into the living room wakened him. When his eyes popped open, their sleep-glazed appearance and his honest surprise at seeing them convinced the boys that he hadn't been back in the stone field playing a trick on them.

Even more than playing the joke itself he loved to crow about how successful he'd been in tricking them. If it wasn't their dad in the field, what or who was it?

The boys picked up their camping gear the next morning. The rest of the summer they camped on the other side of the farm.

Even now, several years after they saw the glowing figure in the stone field they can't explain just what it was they saw that night.

 When asked if he camped in the stone field now with his kids, Jim replied, "Well, I don't reckon there's anything back there that would hurt you, but there's some other spots on the farm that make mighty nice campsites.

CHAPTER IX

THE SOCIABLE GHOST

erhaps the most sociable ghost I heard of in Door County was Captain Gust. Christened Gustav Josef Anders as a baby in his native Sweden and born into a seafaring family, it was to be expected that Gust would follow his father and brothers to the sea. It's not really clear how Gust happened to settle for a time, in Door County, but while here he built a house, increased his family and captained a ship for the Great Lakes line.

By all accounts, Gust was a handsome figure of a man easily topping six foot with broad shoulders and strongly defined features that broke into a broad smile whenever he was amused, which was often.

Gust loved foot stomping music, but his wife always accused him of not being able to carry a tune if his life depended on it. Gust would grumble about not getting any respect from his wife, but everybody knew that pretty little blond Anna Marie was the apple of Gust's eye.

For his Annie and their ever-increasing brood, Gust built a large, white house just outside of town on  Washington Island. Whenever Gust was home, laughter and music could be heard through windows opened to catch a breeze.

As times changed, Gust and his family moved on to follow his work. First to Milwaukee and then on to California where Gust eventually died as an old man, but later day owners of his island home suspect that Gust never forgot just how much he loved his Door County years.

Jack and Betty Lucas purchased the old Anders place when the chance presented itself for them to leave the rat race and traffic of Chicago to run a small business on the island.

They moved into the house on a Sunday, and on Monday Jack headed off to work and the two children to school. Betty was left home with Pogo, the family's terrier, to attack the mountain of packing boxes.

About mid-morning, Betty was arranging bedding and towels in the upstairs linen closet when she heard a friendly laugh at the base of the stairs.

Thinking that a neighbor had come to call she dusted off her pants, straightened her hair, and went down the steps to welcome her first visitor.

When Betty got to the bottom of the steps no one waited to greet her. She called a hello but got no answer. Betty was perplexed having been sure that she had clearly heard a man's laugh only moments before.

Pogo however was more angry than perplexed. The small dog stood in the center of the dining room growling and barking loudly in the direction of the bay windows.  Betty searched the downstairs and finding nobody in the house returned to her unpacking chores.

Over the next few months, Betty occasionally heard the unexplained laughter, but it wasn't until the family purchased a piano and put it in the dining room that Jack began to take her seriously when Betty talked about the odd noises.

In the middle of the night long after both children and parents had gone to bed, Jack was wakened by a tentative plunking on the piano. Thinking one of the youngsters was doing a little late night practicing, he nudged Betty awake. The erstwhile musician hit a few more disjointed notes as they listened.

Pogo, sleeping at the end of the bed, awoke with a start and raced down the carpeted hallway as fast as his short legs could carry him barking loudly every step of the way.

When Jack and Betty reached the dining room, Pogo was yipping angrily at an empty piano stool. A quick check revealed both children still sleeping soundly.

This pattern was repeated frequently over the next few months. Finally even Pogo didn't rush out to bark every time their midnight musician began tinkling the piano keys.

In fact, after several years of late night music, the family failed to notice the noise. However, overnight friends of the children were amazed and a little frightened whenever it happened.

After first hearing the midnight serenade, Kelly's best friend swore that she'd never sleep there again, but she soon forgot her vow and a few weeks later was once again sleepily talking with Kelly when the plunking on the piano keys began. Since Kelly wasn't frightened the girl covered her head with a pillow and pretended that she couldn't hear anything.

This story being before the days of TV trays and microwave dinners on the run, the family gathered most evenings around the big oak table in the dining room for the evening meal.

Shortly after the antique rocker was placed in front of the bay windows, Betty noticed that the chair would often rock slightly while the family ate. Much speculation was made about air currents, and so forth, but nobody really came up with an explanation.

A few weeks later, Betty began seeing a vague form in the chair. Shortly after, the form was identifiable as a ruggedly handsome man dressed in an old-fashioned sailor's coat and cap.

Soon both Betty and Kelly could cearly see a smiling man sitting in the rocker. The male half of the family saw the chair rock, but could not see the figure sitting in it.

After doing some research into the history of the

house, the family dubbed their friendly ghost Captain Gust with Betty and Kelly insisting that the apparition in the rocker resembled the photo of Gustaf Anders that they had.

Their extra guest never caused any mischief in the house beyond his love of music although Pogo never reconciled himself to its appearance, barking whenever it was about.

Betty hinted that the ghost of Captain Gust seemed a very sociable sort often appearing when the family had company for dinner. Captain Gust would rock gently while following the conversation at the table by turning his head to watch the person speaking.

About seventeen years after moving into the house the family undertook a remodeling project. They modernized the kitchen, closed a back stairway, rearranged furniture, and painted the dining and living rooms. Evidently Captain Gust didn't like the color of the new paint or objected to the disruption of his quiet home. He disappeared and never returned.

Captain Gust must have been an ideal guest because with a little shrug Betty admitted that she rather missed him.

CHAPTER X

THE LONESOME WORKER

 hey always whispered that Grandma Wetterstra was a little "tetched" in the head after Gramp died. They'd cover their smiles and roll their eyes when she started talking about how she'd talked to Grandpa Wetterstra the night before.

Grandma always said that Gramp came in about the same time as he finished evening chores when he was still alive.

Then she'd shake her head in puzzlement and "tsk, tsk" about whether even now that he was dead and buried he was working as hard as he did when he was alive.

According to Grandma, Gramp's ghost liked to sit in his favorite chair by the fire and rock while she told him about what all had happened since the last time he was there.

 One time Cousin Ralph claimed that he saw the chair rocking and that even though he didn't see anybody in it that Grandma Wetterstra said that Gramp was tired that night but came by to catch up on the news anyway.

Grandma and Grandpa homesteaded their place in Moonlight Bay back in the early days. Grandpa built her the little house first; then when the babies started coming, he built the big house across the yard.

When Uncle Oscar, their middle boy, got married and took over the farm, he moved into the big house and Grandma and Grandpa moved back into the little one.

The big house is still there, but the little one slowly rotted away after Grandma died. An old pump stands in the yard yet, and a few boards, mostly covered by grass, mark the spot where the house once stood.

Some years back, Uncle Oscar gave up farming, packed up his family, and moved away. He tried to rent the big house, but It was hard to find somebody that would put up with living in such an isolated spot especially in the winter when skis were of more use than a car. Most summers somebody new moved into the house.

The summer they did all the work on the highway north from Sturgeon Bay a group of men on the road crew rented Uncle Oscar's house.

After a particularly hot day, the men drove in to Bailey's Harbor to cool off in their favorite bar over cold beers and a game of pool. A couple of the guys stayed home, though, and the hot, still air in the house soon drove them out onto the hammock and chairs on the porch to catch a cool breeze.

While they were talking the sun set; but soon a glorious full moon lit the yard and buildings. The ramshackle little house stood not far from where the two sat, and a movement in that direction caught their attention.

The figure of an old man moved across the yard from the direction of the dilapidated little house.

In the moonlight, the man's weathered face and flowing white hair and beard were clearly visible.

The two men on the porch realized at the same time that though the figure had a definite shape,  it also had no substance. The lines of the old house, the pump handle, even the un-mown grass were visible through his body.

The two didn't stay around long enough to see where the figure went or what it did. By unspoken agreement, they leapt to their feet, ran to the pickup and drove to town. After a cool drink to steady their shaking nerves, they were soon re-counting their experience to their doubting buddies.

The little house is gone now, but I sometimes wonder if Grandpa Wetterstra still stops by to rest a spell and catch up on what's happened since he was last there.

CHAPTER XI

THE PEANUT BUTTER BANDIT

iss Emma was one of those people who took in strays. She lived on a little piece of ground at the edge of Egg Harbor. Just out of high school, she went away to teacher's college and came back certified to teach in one of the many local single-room school houses.

Even as a youngster, Emma was considered a bit odd and as she aged she became rather a local character. As a teacher, she was a great favorite with her students because of her unusual approach to education but often found herself at cross purposes with the school fathers that favored a more traditional classroom. As a result, Emma found herself teaching in several different schools in the course of her short career. Perhaps this or the general attitude that married ladies weren't suitable as teachers ended her career in education.

Despite the fact that Emma did marry, she remained Miss Emma to the countless students who had the unique experience of being in her classroom. It was always said that Miss Emma's marriage was more a result of her habit of taking in strays than a love match, but whatever the beginning she and Oscar shared better than forty years of living beneath the weathered shingles of Emma's slope-roofed cottage.

Shortly after, Emma inherited a small cottage from her widowed father. Oscar, an out-of-work cooper displaced by a drop in fishing, showed up at  Emma's back step looking for work. Some said the reason Oscar was out of work was because he couldn't make a watertight barrel, not because barrels weren't needed, but Miss Emma always pooh poohed any slander of Oscar's abilities. Although it was that very lack that brought them together.

Miss Emma hired Oscar to reshingle the leaky roof of her cottage, and Oscar to his credit did get better than half the shingles on the roof before disaster struck. He slipped climbing the ladder breaking his ankle in the resulting fall. Of course, Miss Emma with her soft heart for an injured or hungry stray insisted on nursing Oscar back to health.

By the time Oscar's ankle mended, Miss Emma had finished shingling the cottage, resigned from teaching, and she and Oscar were married since it wasn't seemly for an unmarried lady to share a roof, no matter how leaky it might be, with a man.

Over the years, Miss Emma continued taking in strays. Countless half-starved cats and dogs slunk in to feed at the big metal pans on the back steps.

Most stayed to grow fat and tame. A neighbor's lame milk cow took up residence in the shed and refused to stay at home within her own rock fence. Sick birds were nursed back to health, and countless squirrels feasted on peanuts temptingly placed on the kitchen window sill.

It was the peanuts that caused the only serious disagreement between Oscar and Miss Emma. It was generally accepted that Miss Emma spoke her mind and Oscar agreed with her, for kind-hearted Miss Emma could weild a razor-sharp tongue when somebody dared to differ with her.

His peanuts were Oscar's pride and joy. How he managed to raise a crop in an unsuitable climate and ground that was more rock than dirt was never known, but spring after spring Oscar planted his peanuts and come fall he'd go to the garden patch with a five-tined pitchfork and come back after hours of coaxing the rocky ground to give up its tender crop with more peanuts than Miss Emma knew what to do with.

One especially bountiful year Miss Emma, never one to let food go to waste, decided to try out a new idea she'd read about the winter before. Unfortunately she couldn't find the article so she had to work from memory.

Miss Emma ground a big batch of peanuts, mixed in a host of other ingredients, spread the concoction on bread and offered it to Oscar for lunch. Oscar took  one bite and pronounced it unfit for eating.

Miss Emma was disappointed, but having had an advance taste herself secretly agreed with Oscar. She set that batch in the root cellar and continued to experiment until finally Oscar said, "Miss Emma, this is delicious. You may butter my bread with it any day." Miss Emma took him at his word, and it became Oscar's standard lunch.

There was a long line of jars in the root cellar before Miss Emma developed the recipe that Oscar approved of. The jars stood neglected and forgotten in the cool cellar all that winter.

The next spring an inquisitive baby raccoon wandered into the yard. A recent stray dog not used to the "live and let live" attitude Miss Emma enforced chased the youngster up the new electric light pole sitting in the yard.

Aroused by the barking, Miss Emma hurried from her afternoon nap in the sitting room to the kitchen door. She reached the back step as the raccoon clambered to the top of the pole. The unfortunate baby managed to put his feet in all the wrong places. The current jolted through his tiny body making all of his fur stand on end, and with a yelp he fell to the ground.

As Oscar came running from the barn to see what caused the racket, Miss Emma scooped up the unmoving bundle of charred fur and headed for her kitchen throwing over her shoulder, "I told you nothing good would come of that new-fangled electricity. We got along just fine without it! Look at this poor baby. He's half fried and barely breathing."

Miss Emma nursed the pitiful little creature back to health. She tended his burns and forced milk teaspoon by teaspoon down his throat until he finally began eating on his own. Under her watchful eye, he began playing about on the floor, grew new fur, and became a pampered pet. By the end of the summer, the raccon was fully recovered and full-grown.

He had a glossy coat marred only by being short half his right ear and some toes on his right hind foot. Miss Emma insisted when Oscar poked fun at his appearance that it made him look like a pirate or a bandit.

As the raccoon's health improved, Oscar's troubles began. "Oscar! Oscar! Come quick and bring the ladder. Raccoon has got himself up the tree again and can't get down."

Ladder in hand Oscar approached the tree for the third time in as many days, "If that beast bites me again today, it's the last time I'll be getting him out of anything. I think that electricity addled his brain. What's he go climbing the tree for if'n he can't get down?" Muttering under his breath, Oscar continued, "Dang fool animal is the worst thing that ever happened around here. He's more trouble than all the rest together."

From the bottom of the ladder, Miss Emma scolded, "You're just out of sorts, Oscar, because I made them take that pole away. We don't want that kind of thing here, half killing innocent animals."

Now whether it was the removal of Oscar's coveted electric pole or the fact that the mischievous raccoon always seemed to be causing trouble, the truth was that Oscar could not abide the raccoon.

As far as Oscar could see, the only good to come of the whole incident was that the beast loved the early peanut spread failures that Miss Emma had unsuccessfully tried out on Oscar.

Unfortunately once the animal had eaten all of the rejected jars from the root cellar that wasn't the end of it. The raccoon begged for and received pieces of bread spread with the good recipe of the peanut mix as often as Oscar himself. Oscar had to share his favorite food with an animal he particularly disliked.

Oscar's one small joy was watching the raccoon eat the sticky food. It clung to the roof of his mouth, and he went through all kinds of gymnastics in the process of trying to lick it off, even to the point of sommersaulting off the cabinet if he got a particularly large mouthful. The thud of his well-padded, furry body hitting the floor gave Oscar a perverse satisfaction. "Serves you right you, little thief," Oscar would mutter.

 It wasn't uncommon for Oscar to come into the kitchen complaining about the raccoon's latest mischief, "Emma! Emma! Where are you? That beast has been in my garden again! He stripped three ears of sweet corn and then didn't even eat any of it. When I get my hands on him. . ."

"Now, Oscar, how do you know it was Peanut? There's plenty of wild raccoons in the timber that could have done it."

"Not with just two toes on their back right foot. I saw his tracks in the mud just as plain as I'm standing here," Oscar insisted.

"Well, I'm sure he didn't mean any harm, Oscar. I'll talk to him about it. Why don't you go out to the root cellar and bring in a jug of cider and I'll fix you a snack.

"She'll talk to him about it. Hmm! Lot of good that will do. You can't sweet talk an animal especially not one that doesn't have anything between its ears to think with," Oscar muttered as he went to fetch the cider.

 By the time he returned from the root cellar, the thought of a nice, cool cup of tart cider had improved Oscar's temper. One look at the muddy tracks with a distinctive two-toed hind paw print that led to the kitchen table had Oscar yelling, "Emma!"

Peanut, the raccoon, sat perched on Oscar's chair holding a sandwich, Oscar's sandwich, between his front paws greedily stuffing bites of it into his mouth. Oscar slammed the cider jug on the wooden cabinet and stomped out of the kitchen muttering, "I'll not have a moment's peace until the animal is gone." Oscar was wrong. He didn't have a moment's peace even when Peanut was gone.

Much to Oscar's chagrin, Peanut lived a long life. Much to Oscar's credit, Peanut died a natural death. Even in his old age, the raccoon delighted in raiding Oscar's garden and stealing peanut sandwiches whenever one was left untended for even a few moments.

Oscar can be forgiven if he didn't show the same amount of grief that Emma did at Peanut's passing. Emma didn't see the smile of satisfaction that briefly crossed Oscar's face as the last shovelful of dirt was tamped onto the raccoon's grave or hear Oscar's muttered, "At last I'm free of that sneak thief!"

Not more than a week later, Emma called from the back step to Oscar, "I'm going to town for groceries. I've a meal for you on the table."

Oscar finished hoeing his row of beans and went to the house for his lunch. He washed his hands at the pump in the kitchen sink and crossed to sit at his place at the table.

"Fool woman, if she was hungry, why didn't she

fix her own sandwich for lunch instead of eating half mine?" Oscar grumbled. He picked up his sandwich, grimaced at the teeth marks, then shrugged his shoulders and finished off the sandwich. "She doesn't even like this peanut spread. Why was she eating my sandwich?"

Oscar was busy in his garden that afternoon and forgot to question Miss Emma about the half-eaten sandwich, but in the course of the next several months, it became a bone of contention between them. More often than not if Miss Emma left a peanut sandwich for Oscar he would complain that she had eaten part of it. Miss Emma, of course, always denied any responsibility insisting that she preferred butter and jam on her bread.

The following summer Oscar came in from a hard morning's work. The boots he left at the door were coated with mud from the previous night's rain and woe betide the man or animal that tracked across Emma's freshly scrubbed floor.

Oscar hung his cap on the peg by the door and glanced at the table to see what lunch might be. Emma's plate held a cheese sandwich and Oscar's plate a peanut spread sandwich with a big chunk nibbled out of the side of it.

Leading across the floor were muddy tracks, raccoon tracks with the hind right foot having only two toes. "Emma!"

They never did explain the mystery. Emma quit making Oscar's sandwiches ahead of time, and if she did leave one unwatched, it invariably had a bite ripped out of it. When this happened Oscar carefully used his pocketknife to cut around the teeth marks and ate the rest of the sandwich. No raccoon, dead or alive, was going to cheat Oscar out of his favorite meal.

Eventually both Emma and Oscar passed on and that should have ended it, but it didn't.

"Mom, Sarah ate a bite of a my peanut butter sandwich while I was outside feeding the dog."

"Did not!" answered Sarah. "But if I had, it would have paid you back for eating almost half of mine last week when I was on the phone."

"I didn't eat your dumb sandwich last week. It was chunky peanut butter and I like mine creamy. Just ask Mom".

Over the years in a certain small cottage on the outskirts of Egg Harbor a peanut butter sandwich simply wasn't safe.

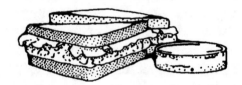

CHAPTER XII

NORTHERN LIGHTS

hope they never change this road, Dad. I like winding around the light poles. It feels like you're driving in a tunnel with the timber so dense on both sides of the road."

Herman grabbed the padded arm rest of the boy's '67 Mustang and clutched it to keep from sliding across the car as his college-age son swung the vehicle around yet another of the curves that mark the northern end of Highway 42. The car headed directly at the electric pole on the opposite side of the road.

"Just don't forget the tree in the middle of the road at the north end, Danny. I want to make it home in one piece to eat that strawberry cake your mother was frosting when we left." The joking reminder was spoken only half in jest. Herman promised himself the next time the two of them went somewhere they'd take his own pickup, with him driving.

"Hey, look! There's a doe and that big buck we saw last fall." The headlights of the car briefly silhouetted two deer standing in the narrow strip of grass along the paved road. The doe leaped the fence immediately, but the buck tossed his heavily antlered head before he jumped gracefully into the timber, quickly vanishing in the darkness.

The car's headlights swung crazily into the trees as the boy tugged the steering wheel to the right to keep the buck in sight a few moments longer. The white line around Herman's mouth grew even tenser, and his blunt fingernails dented the vinyl arm rest.

The car topped the last little rise in the road, swerved to the right avoiding the tree growing between the north and south bound lanes, and slid to a stop with its nose pointed haphazardly at Pilot Island. On the driver's side, the Coat Guard dock stretched out toward Plum Island. The sound of waves lapping on the rock-strewn white sand beach to the east was the only sound. The few lights visible on Washington Island seemed dim in comparison to the bright stars glittering overhead.

"Northport never changes much, does it?" It was more of an observation than a question. "There aren't any fisherman tonight."

"There were probably plenty of them earlier. They've been catching quite a few fish off here this summer."

The two car doors slammed in unison as with unspoken consent both father and son climbed out of the car and walked the length of the cement dock. "The ferry come in over here much this winter, Dad?" Danny questioned idly.

With a shake of his head, the older man answered, "Not as much as some years. It was a mild winter and they could get into the dock at Gills Rock. Some say they ought to straighten the road and fix up the dock here and use it all the time, but I don't think they'll ever do that."

The two reached the end of the wide dock and with a shrug of his shoulders Herman leaned back against one of the huge black tires chained as bumpers to the dock pilings. "Some things never seem to change and this place is one of them."

"The stars sure are bright tonight," Danny observed as he sat down on the cool concrete, stretching his legs out in front of him while leaning on another of the thick wooden posts.

"I can remember coming here with your Grandpa when I was younger. This was always one of his favorite places, especially in August when the northern lights were showing."

"Tell me about him," Danny knew that the simple request would unlease a flood of reminiscing. His dad loved to tell a story, and tales of Danny's grandfather were a favorite subject.

"Every year about this time Dad would come into the house and say he reckoned it was about time the two of us walked over to the dock."

"We'd hike the deer trails along the bluff from Wisconsin Bay. When I was younger, it always amazed me how he could find his way through the timber in the dark. I'd slip a light in my pocket and use it if he got ahead of me. Most nights though it was bright like this when we came, and you really didn't need a light once you got used to the dark," Herman paused to settle himself on the dock leaning back against a tire for support while facing out into the lake.

Reflected moonlight danced across the tops of the gently rolling waves. "Dad loved this kind of night. He said it made for a good catch in the next day's fishing," Herman lapsed into silence enjoying the cool evening breeze and the sense of peace that hung over the area. One by one the distant lights on Washington and Detroit islands blinked off until only star light lit the scene.

"Did you just hike over here and then home again in the dark?" Danny questioned.

"Yes, that's pretty much what it was," Herman agreed with a shrug. "I guess maybe your Grandpa knew about quality time before all the fancy psychologists put a label on it. He was always busy

between fishing and working as a carpenter, but he found time to take us boys off by ourselves. Sometimes he'd talk, but most times he'd just listen while I rattled on about school or my latest girl problems."

With a chuckle Danny admitted, "I can't imagine you ever having girl problems, Dad."

"Believe it, boy, and the worst of them was your mama. She put me through all kinds of misery before she finally agreed to marry me. It was right here on this very spot that your grandpa told me to quit being such a fool and propose to her before somebody else did. That same night we saw the most impressive display of northern lights I've ever seen."

"I've never seen them," Danny said wistfully.

"It's been a few years since I've seen them myself. Your grandpa seemed to have a sixth sense for knowing when they were going to be. I can't remember even one time that he brought me out here that we didn't see at least a small showing. It's too bad he died before you were born. The two of you would have liked each other," Herman adjusted into a different position on the cooling cement and a comfortable silence spread between father and son.

"Look a shooting star," Danny pointed out over the bay to the bright white streak cutting across the night sky. Danny cleared his throat nervously and then began, "Uh, Dad, it's kind of odd that you mentioned proposing to Mom earlier. Michelle and I've been dating for over a year now, and I really love her and . . .," his voice trailed to silence.

"In your own round about way, son, are you trying to tell me you proposed to Michelle?" Herman questioned.

 "Well, not yet, Dad," Danny admitted. "I know she likes me and all that, but you don't think she'd say 'no', do you?"

Danny's uncharacteristic hesitancy brought a smile to his father's face. "No, I don't think she'll turn you down, and I'll give you the same advice that your grandpa gave me." Herman continued in a reassuring voice. "Quit wasting time and give her a ring before someone else does. She's a fine girl and will make a good wife. That's exactly what your grandpa said about your mama and I'm sure that's what he'd say about Michelle if he were still alive."

"Thanks, Dad," Danny responded to his dad's support. Then, as his stomach growled, he questioned in a lighter tone, "Do you suppose that cake's frosted yet?"

"Yep, I reckon so, and if we want any of it we'd best get home before your brothers finish off every crumb. It's all your mother can do to keep those two fed," Herman stood up and turned to retrace his steps to the car.

"Dad, look!"

As they watched, a greenish glow brightened the northern sky. Streaks of orange and pink flamed from the water spreading across the night sky until the entire landscape was lit by flowing, flaring tongues of intense color.

Every tree on the distant islands was silhouetted by the flaming colors in the northern sky, and the rolling waves of the Door Passage reflected each vibrant streak of pink and gold; and then almost as fast as it appeared the gold glow diffused. White stars glimmered against a black backdrop.

It was a few moments before either Herman or Danny moved or spoke, "Did I really see that, Dad?"

"You really saw that, son. That's the way it was the night your grandpa told me to propose to your mom. It's almost as if he just gave his blessing to you and Michelle." They walked to the car in silence still awed by the spectacular display of northern lights.

As they stepped off the end of the dock and reached the car, Herman's practicality asserted itself. Clutching his pipe between his teeth he suggested, "How about I drive back, Danny. It's been a long time since I've driven your car. I'd like to see how it handles."

"Good try, Dad," Danny replied as he flipped the keys in the air over his father's head and then deftly caught them himself before sliding behind the steering wheel. "You have to live dangerously once in a while! If I can risk proposing to Michelle, you can risk riding with me."

It's been several years since the night Danny and Herman saw the spectacular display of aurora borealis from the Northport dock. Change has come in many forms. The ferries land regularly at the enlarged dock, the road from Gill's Rock to Northport has been straightened, and Danny and Michelle have children of their own now.

Some things haven't changed. Herman still clutches the arm rest when Danny is behind the wheel of a car. Danny hasn't seen the northern lights since that August night when his father passed along the grandfather's wise advice. Even today a trip to the Northport dock after dark has him searching the sky. Was it just coincidence or was there some special meaning to seeing the lights that particular night?

(87)

CHAPTER XIII

THE HOUSE ON GEORGIA STREET

 eorgia Street in Sturgeon bay looks like the typical peaceful tree-shaded city street. Occasionally kids testing their driving skill on the S-curve midway up the street from the bay squeal their tires breaking the serenity of the landscape, but overall the street lives up to its quiet appearance.

The old houses are well-kept. Each looks much like the house sitting next door, but according to one former owner a house not far from the curve contains an unwelcome ghostly resident.

The house is old, by one account dating back some 130 years to the early days of Sturgeon Bay. Despite its modest appearance, it's a big place containing five bedrooms and comes complete with damp, spooky basement and cobwebby attic.

Paul Lutz lived next door as a boy and can

remember his neighbors digging up bones in the back yard. The people always assumed they had dug into an old Indian burial and didn't think much of it. Paul's not so sure now that the bones should have been disturbed.

Paul and Helen bought the Georgia Street house shortly after their fifth child was born. Five children under one roof create a lot of noise. The Lutzes theorize that since the latest owners, a couple with only one child still at home, haven't been bothered by the ghost that the ghost simply didn't like sharing his space with such a large, loud family.

Helen Lutz is the first to admit that the Georgia Street house was usually lively. The five Lutz children always had friends home for supper or

to stay the night. Paul's been heard to comment that he never worried if he bumped into a strange child raiding the refrigerator. He just figured it was one of the strays that his kids dragged in.

When the Lutzs moved into the Georgia Street house, Paul, Helen, and the baby slept downstairs. The older children shared three of the upstairs rooms. The small, unheated room over the kitchen was set aside as a play area.

The room was once the work room of a harness marker and cobbler, a man who reportedly valued his privacy and became irate if his work was interrupted.

Over the next couple of years the entire family often heard footsteps and other noises coming from the playroom when nobody was in the upstairs of the house.

The odd occurrences weren't limited to this one room, however. The list of the odd happenings that occurred during the twenty years that the Lutzes lived in the Georgia Street house is lengthy.

One winter Helen, the only one home, was sitting in the living room crocheting. The rocker on the far side of the room began swaying. It rocked gently for five minutes while Helen sat spellbound and then it simply quit. Another time while the family was eating supper, the exhaust fan over the stove clicked on and began running.

One spring afternoon Helen was napping in one of the upstairs bedrooms. She was wakened by a firm slap on her rump. The house was empty. The children were at school, and Paul was working at the ship yards. Helen recalls that even after she was completely awake she could still feel the stinging sensation.

In later years, the middle Lutz daughter had a television in her room. Several times she woke in the night to find her TV on and the nearby wastebasket tipped over.

Two incidents concerning the cobbler's old room stand out in the family's memory. When the baby got big enough for a room of his own, the playroom was converted to his bedroom. When the oldest boy, Bill, was home visiting with his wife Michelle, they used young Mike's room.

Because of a headache, Michelle had gone upstairs in the early afternoon to lay down. Bill was sitting in the kitchen about 3:0 p.m. talking to his dad when they heard footsteps in the room above the kitchen. Bill went upstairs to see if Michelle's headache was gone. When he entered the room, Michelle was sound asleep on the bed. in the corner, between the two windows, he saw a vague, stooped figure of a person. As he watched, the shadowy form slowly disappeared.

When Mikey began talking, he told stories about the nasty man in his room. His parents credited his tales to his active imagination and didn't pay too much attention to his stories until he came into their room late one night.

Three-year-old Mike crept up to his sleeping mother and tapped on her shoulder to wake her. Tears were streaming down his face as he sobbed, "He's sitting on my bed and won't let me crawl in. I don't like him. Make him go away."

Slowly the whole story come out. Mikey had gotten up to get a drink of water; and when he came back, the mean man in his room wouldn't let him back in his bed.

Helen took the trusting toddler back to his room and asked if the man was still there. Mikey replied, "Yes, Mommy, tell him to go away and let me sleep."

Feeling a bit foolish but willing to try anything, Helen scolded the invisible figure, "Get off that bed right now and quit scaring Mikey. You ought to be ashamed of yourself going around frightening a little boy."

Mikey piped up, "He's gone now, Mommy." The little boy climbed into bed and was asleep almost instantly.

With an embarrassed shrug of her shoulders, Helen related that the next day she went clear through the house scolding the ghost for scaring Mikey and telling him to quit it.

Although Mikey occasionally mentioned seeing the figure in his room, he was no longer frightened by it.

With their family raised, the Lutzes no longer needed such a big home. They sold the house on Georgia Street and moved to a smaller place.

CHAPTER XIV

THE INN

here are a host of inns in Door County, and each likes to claim superiority over the rest for one reason or another. While one prides itself on quaint decorating, another might boast the tastiest breakfasts and yet another points out its scenic setting. None of them, however, are overly proud of a resident ghost. Yet, more than one person has recounted odd occurrences that happened while they were staying in a Door County bed and breakfast inn. The following tale reportedly happened in the not-too-distant past in one such of these inns.

Helen and her daughter Emily had vacationed for years at the inn. They spent at least one summer weekend in Door County, and most years they planned at least a week's vacation soaking up the sun, searching out the best gift shops, and sampling the food in county restaurants.

An inn in a beautiful tree-shaded location soon became their favorite spot to stay, and they even developed a preference for a certain room. Helen enjoyed opening the windows in their favorite corner room and letting the breeze bring in the sweet scents from the flower garden below the window. The chirping and trills of the birds as dawn broke delighted ears more used to the sound of traffic than bird song.

The year our story begins a college friend of Emily's joined the two in their annual trek to Door County. Helen had the corner room and the two girls were sharing a pretty room down the hall. After unpacking and settling in for their week, Helen slipped on her jogging shoes and headed for the nearby gift shops. The girls set out for the beach.

The three enjoyed a delightful vacation. The girls acquired enviable tans, and Helen found a gift shop with unique handwork and unbelievable prices.

All three were having a great time so it was in the spirit of teasing when during dinner in Egg Harbor Emily accosted her friend Sara, "Hey, I thought we agreed the right side of the dresser top was mine. I've got enough stuff of my own without you piling all your junk there, too."

In a light voice Sara shot back, "What do you

mean? I haven't been putting my stuff on your side. You keep using my stuff and then lay it down with yours, and I have to search for hours to find my eye shadow mixed in with all that gunk you wear."

"Girls, girls, girls," Helen interrupted laughingly, "If you'd pay attention to what you're doing instead of thinking about boys all the time, you wouldn't have these problems."

The conversation probably would have been forgotten except when they got back to the inn that evening Sara's comb and make-up was once again mixed in with Emily's. Both girls were certain that their things had been neatly divided when they left the room.

The next few days they made a point of noting the placement of things on the dresser when they left the room. More often than not when they returned the things would be moved.

Wednesday morning Sara ripped the covers off Emily's sleeping body and began tickling her.

"That's for forgetting to turn off the light last night when you finished reading!"

Emily slid off the bed and rolled up in the quilt from the bed to protect her ticklish sides. Once she quit giggling she asked, "What do you mean? I finished my chapter and went to bed just after you. I turned the light off when I came back from the bathroom."

"Are you sure you didn't forget? The light woke me up about two."

Emily shook her head being certain that she had turned the lamp off.

Two nights later Sara poked Emily gently in the ribs, "Emily? Emily? Are you awake?"

A groggy "Hmm" was her answer.

"Wake up, Emily. The light's on again. Did you turn it on?"

"Huh, what? Huh-uh, I went to sleep before you did, remember?"

Just then, the girls heard the soft click of the door closing. "That was the door!"

Both girls jumped out of bed and ran to the corridor. Emily reached the paneled wood door first and tried to jerk it open. The door refused to open and Sara reached around her to flip the interior bolt open. With Sara peering over her shoulder, Emily quickly swung the door open.

The figure of a young woman, her long hair pulled back from her face, disappeared around the corner to the stairs as they watched. Her loose white dress swirled around her hurrying feet.

Emily slumped against the door frame and looked at Sara, "Did you see that?"

"Err, you mean the girl?" When Emily nodded, Sara hesitated and then continued. "Did you notice anything . . . a . . . odd about her?"

"You mean other than that she was in our room when I bolted the door before we went to bed?"

"Oh, Emily!" Sara said in exasperation. "Quit teasing! Could you see through her? I mean you could see her, but you could see the flowered wallpaper and the furniture behind her too, couldn't you?"

"Yeah."

Needless to say, the two girls didn't get much sleep that night. When they recounted their experience to Helen the first thing the next morning, Helen thought they were just teasing. However, Emily's insistence that they weren't kidding and their obvious reluctance to spend the next night in the room convinced her.

Helen and Emily still stay at the inn. They request the corner room. Two different times while they've been there in the last few years the person staying in the room down the hall has mentioned finding the light on at night. As far as they know no one else has seen the girl in the hall, but then that isn't the kind of thing most people would admit to seeing.

CHAPTER XV

SOPHIA'S ROOM

ophia was an attractive girl by all reports. She set great store in her beauty and with the aid of her daddy's money to purchase the newest in skin creams and the most fashionable clothes from the catalog she was considered one of the more elegant young ladies in Door County in the early 1900's.

Of course, it was not chance that the young man selected as her fiance was a handsome up-and-coming officer on the Goodrich Steamship Line.

Some said Stanley, a nice young man by all accounts, was truly in love with the somewhat spoiled Sophia. Others, more cynical in their opinions, suggested that Stanley was more smitten with his future father-in-law's money than his willful bride.

Although she was correct, Sophia was far too prone to point out what a handsome couple she and Stanley made with their dark good looks complementing each other. This preoccupation with outward appearances may have begun all of Sophia's troubles.

All summer Sophia and her mother had been making preparations for her July wedding. Sophia's dress, hand sewn by Miss Maggie, the finest seamstress in all of Door County, hung in the huge oak wardrobe in her room, and Sophia was dreamily anticipating her wedding trip to Chicago.

In preparation for the wedding, the stone house not far off what is now Highway 42 was polished from floor boards to rafters.

A high-backed dresser was added to the furniture in Sophia's sunlit room since the happy young couple planned to make their home with the bride's parents for a time.

As the day of the wedding approached, Sophia was a bundle of nerves. In less than a week she would be married to her handsome Stanley. She fretted about whether there would be enough food for the wedding guests, about her hair, about whether Stanley would remember to polish his shoes, and a whole host of inconsequential details.

When the young cousin dispatched to watch for the arrival of Stanley's ship raised the alarm that he could see it on the horizon, Sophia fretted at leaving all of her little jobs undone to walk down to the dock. Nevertheless, being a truly devoted bride, Sophia rushed down to the dock to meet the steamer.

Alas, her beloved Stanley did not disembark. The captain had a message for Sophia from Stanley. He related that the brave Stanley had been burned in a boiler accident aboard ship. One crewman had died and Stanley had been badly burned saving another. Stanley, although his life was not in danger, was hospitalized in Chicago and would remain so for some time.

Sophia's immediate reaction was to book passage on the next ship headed south that she might comfort her injured Stanley. She might have done so had not a young cabin boy accosted her as she left the ship.

The lad graphically described the accident and the painful burns suffered by Stanley summing up by saying, "He shore look'd awful what with them burns all over and his hair all charred off. I'd not recognized him if'n I didn't know who it was. Why he didn't even sound like hisself. His voice being all croaky with the smoke and all."

Sophia didn't stay around to hear any more.

Her delicate stomach was lurching violently and clapping a hand over her mouth, Sophia fled the ship.

The thought of her handsome Stanley so badly disfigured that she'd not recognize him was more than Sophia could bear. She retired to her room and stayed there for days refusing to speak to anybody and rousing herself only to eat.

Whether Sophia's depression was caused by the thought of the agony suffered by her beloved Stanley or the thought that his handsome appearance would never be the same, you will have to decide for yourself.

Sophia had led a very sheltered life. Perhaps we shouldn't be too harsh in judging her reluctance to attend at Stanley's sickbed. Whatever the reason, Sophia adamantly refused her family's offer to travel with her to Chicago to visit the hapless Stanley, who through messages conveyed by his fellow workers on the steamship line desperately desired to see his beloved bride-to-be.

After more than a week had passed, a written message arrived from Stanley. It began, "My

Dearest Sophia, I await your arrival. The balm of your sweet smile and tender touch will speed my recovery so that we may be married soon. Yours always, Stanley."

Sophia replied, "My poor Stanley, I can not bear to see you in pain or think of your horrible burns. I await your return when you have recovered. Your loving Sophia."

Messages passed back and forth with Stanley pleading for Sophia's attendance at his bedside and Sophia steadfastly refusing to go to him, but maintaining her love and devotion.

In her final message Sophia declared, "My dearest Stanley, I count the days until you are well enough to return to me. I can not bear to leave the house knowing you are still in pain. I stay in my room, the room we will soon share, dreaming of your coming. I shall wait for you forever." Your loving Sophia.

Evidently Stanley had had enough of his reluctant bride. His final message to Sophia read, "You may wait forever.   Stanley."

Word filtered up from Chicago that Stanley had married his nurse at the hospital and though slightly scarred was still a handsome man and a well-respected ship's officer.

Sophia, whether through vanity at being jilted or true depression, secluded herself in her upstairs room. As the years passed and she refused to resume a normal life, her heart became as cold as the brown stone walls that surrounded her.

Her room remained as it had been in preparation for Stanley's coming. The finely carved wardrobe stood on one wall. A carefully pressed and yellowing wedding dress hung inside.

A lady's dresser with its compliment of powders, brushes, and scent bottles stood to one side of the curtained window while on the other side stood the empty highboy dresser, waiting to be filled with Stanley's manly possessions.

Sophia slept alone beneath a lace coverlet in the tall bed dreaming of the day that her beloved Stanley would return. Despite the tender care shown by her loving family, Sophia was never the same. She never left the stone house, seldom left her room, and firmly insisted that Stanley would return for their wedding as soon as he was able.

A picture of the two of them stood on her dresser as a daily reminder of their everlasting love, and Sophia stood at her window by the hour watching for Stanley's ship to dock.

Sophia refused to change even the smallest thing in her room insisting that it was perfect for Stanley just as it was. When spring cleaning was finished, every piece of furniture was replaced in exactly the same location. The dresser remained empty in preparation for Stanley's clothing.

Twenty spring cleanings came and went before Sophia faded away. Some said that she died of a broken heart finally admitting to herself that Stanley would not return. The doctor wrote influenza on her death certificate, but perhaps heart failure might have been more accurate. Even at the end, though, with her last breath, Sophia declared her undying love for Stanley and pledged to wait for him forever, if necessary.

Now, that should have been the end of Sophia's tragic tale, but some familiar with her old house say differently. The house still stands. Its weathered stones look much the same as when Sophia lived. The trees are taller, the grass better kept, and the kitchen remodeled, but some things, to the current owner's chagrin, remain the same.

Distant relatives own the house now. A few of the antiques have been removed over the years, but upstairs in Sophia's room the same bed, wardrobe, and dressers remain. A few years back, an attempt was made to remove the wardrobe, but it was returned to the room when it was found to be virtually impossible to maneuver it down the narrow enclosed stairway.

Sophia's wedding dress and her picture of Stanley were long ago packed away in a trunk in the attic, but the furniture remains as Sophia placed it. It's easier that way.

Sophia's ghost has never been sighted, but some very odd occurrences would lead even the slightly superstitious to believe that Sophia is still making her presence felt. As long as the furniture in her old bedroom remains in Sophia's chosen locations, life is quiet in the stone house. Should the room be rearranged things begin going "bump' in the night.

Helen, a recent owner of the house, dusted and aired Sophia's old room when a young niece was invited for the Christmas holidays. In the process of cleaning the room, she decided to move the highboy to a different wall.

The niece arrived that night, unpacked her clothes hanging the dresses in the wardrobe and placing the rest in the newly moved dresser.

She passed a peaceful night in Sophia's room and attended church the next day with the family. Returning from the services she ran up to her room to change before dinner.

When she opened the door to her room, the big dresser lay toppled across the bed with her few possessions scattered across the floor. The men were called to right the dresser and place it back against the wall.

Three days later the poor girl entered the room to find her things once again strewn across the floor and the dresser leaning against the bed. The dresser was moved back to its original location by the window, and the balance of the girl's visit passed without further incident.

Helen's son and his wife moved into the stone

house next. A few months after moving in Carol, Helen's daughter-in-law, hung new lace curtains at Sophia's old window, placed a matching spread on the bed, and put a beautiful handhooked rug that she had found in a gift shop near Ellison Bay on the wood floor.

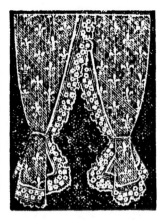

The rug simply didn't fit between the bed and dressers. She called her husband Roy and they began rearranging furniture. By the time Carol was satisfied, virtually every big piece of furniture in the room had been moved.

That night Carol and Roy were wakened shortly after midnight. The scrape of something heavy being dragged across the floor upstairs was followed by a series of thuds as things bounced off the walls onto the floor. A particularly loud bang split the air, and then all was silent.

Roy, convinced that they had a burglar, quickly grabbed a hammer from his tool box and crept up the stairs. Carol, scared witless, trailed behind him determined to reach her young daughters sleeping in one of the other bedrooms upstairs. When they reached the top of the stairs, Carol hurried to her children's room while Roy approached the guest room, Sophia's old room.

Carol scooped the soundly sleeping girls out of the

bed and hurried to the door intending to carry them downstairs. Roy kicked open the door to Sophia's room brandishing his hammer in front of him, daring the intruder to show his face.

The room was a disaster. Not one piece of furniture stood where Carol and Roy had placed it just hours earlier. The big oak wardrobe lay on its side on the floor. Moonlight from the single window cast an eerie glow on its empty interior. One dresser stood in the middle of the room its drawers and their contents spread across the floor. The mattress lay half off the bed with the other dresser leaning drunkenly against the tall, carved bed frame.

There was no intruder in the room, and when Roy searched the house, he could find no sign of forced entry.

The following day the couple straightened the room putting the furniture back in Carol's placement to show off her new rug. That night, long before dawn, they were wakened by the sound of something heavy being dragged across the floor and the thud of falling objects. Carol and Roy rushed upstairs and thrust open the guest room door. Once again the furniture had been moved and the room was a mess.

Heeding Helen's sage advice, the furniture was placed in Sophia's chosen locations the next day. That night there were no strange noises to disturb the family's sleep.

Over the years, Carol occasionally tried moving some of the furniture around in the room, but every time she would find the piece in the middle of the floor or they'd be wakened in the night by strange noises.

Even to this day, the furniture in a certain room of that stone house is carefully shifted back to its original location when the spring cleaning is done, and no matter how enthusiastic the woman of the house becomes about rearranging furniture that upstairs bedroom will not be touched.

CHAPTER XVI

THE REFUGE

ince the tourist popularity of Door County has grown, some of the more caustic local wits have been heard to comment that half the county is for sale and the other half for rent. One of the county's rooms-for-rent has an interesting reputation.

As more people came to Door County to enjoy the scenery, eat, and shop, the need for temporary help blossomed. In a few short years, the shop keepers and the summer help they were employing were caught in a double bind. The businesses couldn't function without the extra employees, but because of the tourist trade the workers, mostly students, couldn't find affordable housing.

To answer this need many restaurants and gift shops converted little used storerooms and upstairs lofts to sleeping quarters for their employees.

(115)

Louise was hired as a waitress early one June and gratefully accepted the offer of a room to rent above the popular restaurant. She was a quiet girl with long, dark hair and large, brown eyes that seemed to welcome friendship even before her quick smile lit her thin face.

Louise soon became popular with the other girls rooming above the restaurant. Being naturally quiet, she was a good listener and readily empathized with her friends latest problems or joys.

It wasn't uncommon to find two or three girls sprawled across Louise's bed or propped up on the oversized pillows stacked on her floor. Louise herself usually sat in the spindle backed rocker that stood by the window with one of her bare feet twisted underneath her while the other swung loosely in front of the chair giving an occasional nudge to the nearby wooden bed frame to maintain a rhythmic rocking.

As the summer progressed, the other girls suspected that something was not quite right with Louise. She quit accepting invitations to accompany the group when they went swimming, to the movies, or out for a night of partying.

She did little more than work her shift and sleep or sit in the rocker by the window in her room. An eight-hour shift that left the other girls complaining about skimpy tips and sore feet exhausted Louise and set her to bed.

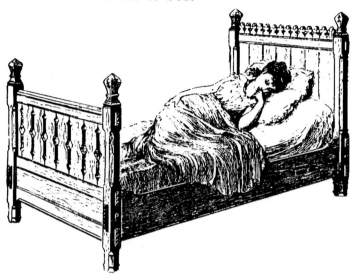

Her worried friends urged Louise to see a doctor. For several weeks, she smiled away their concerns with a plea of a mild virus and assurances that she certainly felt better. That she didn't feel better and was getting weaker by the day was evident to even the most casual observer.

It wasn't until she was forced to cut back her work hours that she confided to her best friend, "I have a rare blood disease. I've been taking different experimental medicines for several years to retard its progress, but it's advanced to the point now where the medicines don't have much of any effect."

Within weeks Louise had to give up her job in the restaurant and rarely had the strength to leave her room. The girls saw to it that she kept her doctor's appointments but could do little else. As their friend's condition worsened and she was unable to do more than sit rocking by the window, they urged her to contact her family.

Louise's reply reflected a lifetime of hurt and rejection. "They know where I am. They send an allowance to cover my living expenses and pay my medical bills directly. I'm sure that my father requests a monthly progress report on my condition."

She continued in a voice that broke slightly with the pain of rejection. "Even before he remarried and I got sick, Father didn't have time for me. I'd be more alone living in their home than I am here in a place I love surrounded by friends." It was one of the few times bitterness crept into Louise's voice.

Occasionally Louise talked about happy, early childhood vacations in Door County with her mother when she had wished that they could stay forever and listen to the sound of waves breaking in the bay and the raucous calls of the gulls when a fishing boat docked.

Mostly Louise sat by the window and quietly rocked, content to soak up the sunshine that filtered through the lacy curtains and to listen to her friends cheery conversations as they stopped by to rest before plunging into their next activity.

Louise was gone before the last days of summer. After two short days in the hospital, she died in her sleep. Even at the end, her family didn't answer the doctor's summons quickly enough to tell her goodbye. Her friends did.

Her father had Louise's few belongings packed and shipped home. Only the memory of Louise's smiling, patient presence remained in the  room that had been her summer home and final refuge.

Early that winter the cook in the now quiet cafe complained that he heard a chair rocking in the room over the kitchen. Although known to be temperamental, he wasn't prone to imagining things so eventually a waitress was dispatched to check out his complaint.

The slightly dusty chair, still placed by Louise's window so she could catch a glimpse of the bay, was indeed slowly rocking. The waitress tugged it away from the window draft and returned to report the problem solved.

A few weeks later the cook again complained about the scraping noise upstairs. Surprisingly, the chair was found by the window again. It was moved to a spot where no draft could possibly affect it.

After the first of the year when the cook, already out of sorts because of arthritic joints, again complained about the noise upstairs, the rocker, found once again by the window, was moved to the hallway outside Louise's room. The rest of the winter passed in peace.

The next spring the rooms above the restaurant were aired out and dusted to be made ready for that summer's renters. Keeping in mind the cook's complaints, the rocker was shoved off to the end of the hall and not returned to the room above the kitchen.

As things go, though, it would happen that the waitress that had the room above the kitchen that summer liked the banished chair and placed it by the window of her room. Once again the rocking

CHAPTER II

THE GLOWING EYES

 young boy, his loose-fitting dun arees rolled up to his knees, sto to tighten his suspenders. Wadii the Horseshoe Bay beach lookii for bits of treasure, broken bright colored glass or shells washed in I last night's storm, turns into an impromptu swi when a big wave catches him. Now his pants a wet and heavy, dragging at his suspenders.

Being a young boy, he's oblivious to the beauty of the long white beach and blue sky. His bare feet squish in the muddy track, and he kicks the top off a rut left by Ole Anderson's wagon.

her friends while she gazed out the window to being the center of attention herself.

Is it a draft from the window that rocks the old chair or the spirit of Louise, content to stay where she found peace and friendship, a sense of belonging, rare in her short life?

CHAPTER XVII

THE SHY GHOST

une Burleigh's husband insisted that she was just upset from the move and was hearing things that first night in their new house, an older frame and brick home located in a quiet residential area of Sturgeon Bay. June shook Thomas out of an exhausted slumber saying she heard a whole group of people talking in the living room.

Now, Thomas Burleigh was a man who took his rest seriously and after cocking his head and hearing nothing, he squinted at his wife and questioned, "You heard somebody breaking in?"

"No," June answered. "It sounds like somebody is having a party in the living room. I hear a group of people talking. You know how it sounds just like a general mumbling when a whole room full of people are talking at the same time? That's what I hear."

Now Thomas had grown up on a farm and worked in the shipyards long enough to have accumulated a colorful vocabulary which he wasn't adverse to using when he thought the situation warranted it. Being wakened in the middle of the night for no apparent reason after a tiring day of moving furniture was enough to upset his already less than calm nature.

June, being used to her husband's lapses, simply covered her ears until he'd calmed down. "I don't hear nothing. You probably left the radio on one of them all night talk shows you're always listening to." Thomas rolled over and promptly began snoring.

June decided to investigate the noise herself, but by the time she reached the top of the steps she no longer heard talking. She nervously descended the stairs hesitating on each step to listen for movement in the darkened rooms below her.

June, her heart beating rapidly, tip-toed through the quiet rooms. The downstairs looked just as it had when the men finished unloading the rental moving truck. Boxes crammed the dining room, and the furniture was haphazardly arranged in the living room leaving little space to even walk through easily. All the doors were secure, the TV and radio were off, and there was no sign of an intruder.

If this had been the only incident June might have agreed with Thomas' assessment that she was just excited from the move and imagining things; but in the several years that the Burleighs lived in the house, other unexplained happenings were commonplace.

One evening when June had a group of ladies for a meeting, one of her friends familiar with the old happenings coaxed, "Hey, June, tell them about your ghost."

June launched into several anecdotes about the odd occurrences in the old house. Just as she related that the ghost, being very conscientious about conserving electricity, turned, the kitchen light off when the room was empty, the kitchen light blinked off.

Some of the ladies began to get a little frightened and it didn't do much to calm their nerves when June said, "Just wait a few minutes and he'll turn it back on." The words had barely left her lips when the kitchen light flicked on.

One friend, prone to scoff at anything remotely supernatural, said, "It's just the wiring. You know how these old houses are."

With a smile June replied, "That's exactly what Thomas said last year before he rewired the kitchen."

The woman that had begun the conversation prompted, "Tell them about the stove and your robe."

"I can't really say that it was the ghost, but one night just as I put my foot on the bottom step of the stairs to go up to bed I saw the fleeting shadow with my side vision that I often see before the kitchen light goes out.

"Anyway, just as I went to go upstairs a feeling hit me that I should check the stove. Now I don't worry about that kind of thing so it was really odd. I went into the kitchen and even before I turned on the light I could see a faint glow.

"The front element was on low. There was a stack of magazines and papers on the counter that I'd gathered to throw away. *The Advocate* had slid off the stack and was laying just a half inch from the hot burner. If I'd gone to bed, I'm sure it would have caught on fire."

Her friend prompted again, "The robe."

"Sometimes things aren't where I leave them. The time I remember the best I had showered before bed. We sleep upstairs, but the bathroom is just off the kitchen down here so I wore my robe up to bed. The living room curtains are tie back so I know I didn't walk through here without my robe!

The next morning when I got up my robe wasn't on the chair or anywhere in the bedroom. When I came downstairs it was hanging on the back of the bathroom door."

"Aren't you scared?" questioned one of the more timid ladies.

After some thought June replied, "Not really. The ghost hasn't tried to hurt us and may have even saved us from a fire. My sister says she's a little frightened when we have her baby sit tne boys but nothing's really happened to scare her. We have had trouble with Jason not sleeping through the night since we moved here though."

At encouraging noises from the rest of the women June continued, "Jason had been sleeping through the night for over a year before we moved, but that first week he started waking up during the night. He still does every so often. He says that there's a man in his room who wakes him.

"Since he's talking better he's described a normal-looking man wearing stripes. We haven't been able to figure out if it's a pinstriped suit or perhaps an old time prison uniform.

"Jason doesn't really seem frightened of the man, just upset because he woke him up. I really am getting tired of getting up to settle him back into bed," June finished with a sigh.

One of the ladies who had been oddly quiet up to this point spoke up, "We had the same problem with a house we used to live in. Something was bothering our little boy at night. My aunt told me to tell the ghost to quit bothering him. I felt a little foolish, but one day while he was in school, I went to his room and did what she said. It worked and he started sleeping through the night and quit talking about the man in his room."

There were a few disbelieving chuckles from the

group, and somebody changed the subject by suggesting they sample June's tasty-looking desserts.

June later said that she really didn't think it would work to scold the ghost, but after another night of waking to calm the Jason at 2:00 A.M., June was ready to try anything no matter how silly it might seem.

The next day, feeling very foolish, June went through every room and closet in the house telling the ghost that she was tired of having it upset her son and that it was to quit bothering the child.

June didn't think much of it when the kitchen light behaved itself and Jason slept through the night the rest of that week. However, a conversation that weekend left June wondering.

That Saturday when Betty, her next door neighbor, stopped in for coffee, Betty began the conversation saying, "If I didn't know better, I'd say your ghost moved in with us."

Our kitchen light has been doing the oddest things all week, and Ruffy has been going nuts barking at nothing. I'll see a shadow out of the corner of my eye and then he'll start barking his head off."

June choked on a mouthful of coffee than asked, "A . . . when did all this start?"

"Let me think," Betty paused thoughtfully taking another sip of her coffee before answering, "It was Wednesday night."

For the rest of the time June and Thomas lived in the house they weren't bothered by temperamental kitchen lights, shadows in the corner, or night-time visitors.

Was the illusive shadow that June had often spotted out of the corner of her eye a shy, sensitive ghost who when scolded about bothering the child moved next door?

CHAPTER XVIII

DOUBLE HAUNTED

cording to the movies and most books, a haunted house is expected to look eerie, be a bit rickety, and have a definite air of mystery about it. There's a house just outside of Sturgeon Bay that does none of the three, yet the people that have lived there for the last twenty years seriously doubt that they are the only "occupants" of the big two-and-a-half-story frame house.

It must follow that since the house doesn't fit the accepted standard for haunted houses that its ghosts wouldn't either. The ghosts seem to be more mischievous than frightening. Perhaps like many Door County natives they're just a little friendlier than what you might run across in other parts of the country.

Shortly after the family moved into the big tree-shaded house, they began to notice strange occur-

rences. It was the children who first complained about missing clothes and toys. When Ellen scolded them with the traditional mother's line, "It's where you left it," it simply wasn't true.

Pamela Sue was a very organized young lady for a fourth grader. Each week night she meticulously laid out her clothes for the next day. Whether prompted by the desire to not keep the school bus waiting or the sibling rivalry of beating her brother Bob to the bathroom, she did it faithfully every night.

Although Bob teased about wanting the bathroom first, he by far preferred laying in bed until the last minute to getting up early. Most days he barely managed to run a comb through his hair and had to rush down the lane, toast in hand, to catch the bus before it pulled away.

On the Tuesday night of the second week of school, Pammy carefully laid out her favorite ruffled white blouse, a pair of tan corduroy knickers, matching socks, and a narrow dark brown ribbon to tie in a bow at the neck of the blouse. She arranged them neatly on the chair by the bed and promptly fell asleep.

(134)

The next morning Pammy popped out of bed, stretched in the bright sunlight coming in the open curtains of her west bedroom, pulled on her pants, buttoned her lacy white blouse tucking it into the waistband of the knickers and sat down on the edge of the rumpled bed to pull on her socks.

The socks weren't on the chair where her other clothes had been. They weren't under the chair. They weren't on or under her bed or on her dresser. She searched under and behind the chair, the bed, and the dresser one more time. She even dug clear through her drawers scattering clothes all over her previously clean room. The socks were simply not there and neither was the dark brown ribbon.

Pamela Sue gulped her breakfast that day and raced down the lane just as the bus pulled off the paved county road into their drive. She wore dark blue knee socks and a navy bow to school that Wednesday.

Two mornings later the socks and ribbon were on the chair by the bed when Pamela Sue opened her eyes and trotted across to the dresser to turn off the alarm clock.

In the next few months, a sweater disappeared one night, a skirt another time, and yet another morning one of her favorite tennis shoes and a belt were gone. Perhaps a few days or sometimes even two weeks later the missing item, clean and neatly folded, reappeared in the same spot that it vanished from.

Now Pamela Sue, being naturally suspicious of her big brother, accused him of playing tricks on her. He'd already received the same lecture from his father and had hotly denied being the prankster. It was only when their mother pointed out that things had disappeared when Bob was staying overnight at a friend's house that he was absolved of suspicion.

It was shortly after that Bob began having the same type of problems. His baseball hat, football, or  model car would vanish from his room only to reappear days or weeks later unharmed in exactly the same spot that it disappeared from.

Only once did the ghost forget to put the item back in the right place. Bob's brand new sleeping bag appeared four weeks after it disappeared in the hay now instead of in his closet.

Bob also complained that someone would come into his room in the middle of the night and bounce on his bed until he woke up. Being just as suspicious of his sister as she was of him, Bob accussed Pammy of playing tricks on him.

After being awakened in the middle of the night for the second time in one week, Bob stamped into Pamela Sue's room to give her a piece of his mind. She was sound asleep.

Most of the odd mischievous activity occurred in the upstairs of the house, but one night after they'd been living in the house for several years the children's father, Paul, wakened shortly after midnight. He got up to go to the bathroom. He and Ellen slept on the first floor of the big house in a room on the west side. From their bedroom, it was necessary to walk through the kitchen to get to the bathroom which was also just off the kitchen.

As he entered the moonlit kitchen, he heard a noise, a small giggle almost, and saw Pammy or her baby sister Janey dressed in a white nightgown scoot around the ironing board set up on the far side of the room and slip into the bathroom ahead of him.

With the weary patience of an experienced father of two little girls, he sank into one of the bentwood chairs at the kitchen table to wait for his offspring to forfeit the bathroom.

Paul waited five minutes, then ten and she still hadn't come out. He tapped on the partially closed door but received no answer. He pushed it open to find the room empty.

Bob might grumble when the ghost bounced on his bed several nights in a row, and the girls complained when favorite toys or clothes disappeared for short stretches of time but since all in all these things seemed more aggravating than frightening. Their mother Ellen can be forgiven if she tended to chalk their problems up to overly active childish imaginations. After all, how many of us want to seriously consider that there might be an extra "something" sharing our living space?

It was a lovely sunny spring day that Ellen was forced to lend some credence to the children's stories. The older two kids were in school. She and Janey, an active three-year-old, were the only ones home. They'd been working in the yard since lunchtime picking up sticks and raking the leaf mulch away from the front and side flower bed.

Ellen heard the beep of the mailman's horn and said, "I'm going to walk down the lane to get the mail, Janey. Do you want to come along?"

The little one shook her heard saying, "I want to play with Muffy."

"O.K., honey. Just don't take the cat into the house. There's meat laid out for dinner."

"I won't, Mommy," Janey promised before darting off to find her pet kitten.

Ellen enjoyed the short stroll down to the mailbox. One side of the lane was open pasture, but the other side had a small timber along it. The Dutchman's britches were in full bloom and a low purple flower was just starting to open. She'd have to look that one up in her wild flower book.

The mail contained the usual assortment of advertising flyers and bills. She tore open the only real letter. It was a short thank-you note from her sister in Escanaba for a birthday present.

As she walked back up to the house, a movement in one of the front bedrooms upstairs caught Ellen's eye. Janey was playing in her sister's room. Ellen muttered to herself, "If she took that cat in and he got into the meat, I'm going to make her explain to her dad why we're having scrambled eggs for supper!"

Ellen stomped around the side of the house clearly expecting a ruined roast in the kitchen. She stopped dead in her tracks. A sleepy-eyed Janey was

 sitting cross legged on the well platform with her back braced against the old but usable pitcher pump. She was humming softly and lightly petting the cat and kitten sleeping nearby.

Whatever or whoever Ellen had seen in Pamela Sue's bedroom it wasn't Janey.

As the kids got older and became involved in school activities, the entire family attended the ball game, concert, or whatever together. More than once as they turned into the lane when they arrived home after dark, the upstairs of the house would be brightly lit.

Of course, the young ones received the "electricity-costs-money" lecture and a reminder to turn off their lights. However, more often than not, by the time the car was parked by the garage, the house was totally dark. All the upstairs lights were off.

As kids will, Bob and Pamela Sue and Janey grew up, tested the winds of independence, and eventually moved out of the big farm house. Ellen, as mothers will, decided to do a bit of redecorating. In the process, the big pool table was banished from the downstairs to a now unused bedroom on the second floor.

The change definitely improved the traffic flow in the downstairs, but it did give rise to renewed speculation about the presence of an uninvited guest in the upper floor of the big white frame home. At the oddest hours of the day and night, balls could be heard rolling about on the table or even jumping the sides and bouncing across the floor.

One hot July afternoon the entire family, Ellen's brother and his family and a neighbor couple were gathered for a Sunday evening picnic in the back-yard.

The men had brought in a big mess of fish and were filleting them on the bench by the back door, the women were gathered in front of the fan in the kitchen to drink tea, snap beans for supper, and catch up on the latest gossip. The children had been drifting between a basketball game out by the garage and the baseball game on T.V.

In a lull in the conversation, Ellen said, "Who's upstairs playing pool? It must be like an oven up there today. The humidity's got the window in that room swollen shut. I haven't been able to get it open all summer."

Bob had just come out to the kitchen for a cold drink and he answered, "Nobody's up there. It got too hot outside so we all came in to see the Brewers whip the Cubs. Unfortunately, the Cubbies are ahead nine to three and it's the bottom of the ninth." he tilted his head and listened to the sound of pool balls rolling across the hardwood floor upstairs and said flippantly, "Must be the ghost, Mom."

Of course, all talk immediately turned to stories of the strange occurrences in the old house over the years. Ellen's sister-in-law said that she'd heard that a former owner's wife had been under psychiatric care at one time because of all the weird things that went on, Ellen's brother brought up the incident with Pammy's boyfriend, and everyone chipped in another odd happening that they remembered.

Finally Ellen slammed her ice tea glass down on the table. "All right, I've had enough of this wild talk. There's no such thing as ghosts. It's just the wind blowing the balls around."

"Right, Mom, and the wind lifts them right off the table, too." As though to punctuate Bob's statement, the sound of three balls being dropped from the height of the table and then rolling across the wood floor was distinctly heard by all in the kitchen.

You could have heard a pin drop in the kitchen as the final ball thudded into a piece of furniture and stopped rolling.

(142)

"Besides, you just said the window in that room won't open."

Ellen preferred not to believe that she had a ghostly inhabitant in her upstairs and was determined to convince everybody, herself included, of that fact. "It's the cat then. Come on and I'll just show you and end all this silly talk once and for all."

She led the way upstairs. When the group reached the top of the steps, the door to the room containing the pool table was securely shut and latched. Ellen pulled it open and called the cat.

There was no answering meow. The room was empty, and all the pool balls were neatly racked on the pool table. Needless to say, Ellen's attempt to end speculation about a ghost in the upstairs only added one more story to the saga.

As the group trailed back to the kitchen, somebody at the back of the line requested, "Tell us about the time Greg saw the little man and that cat, Pam."

Pam shrugged her shoulders and ignoring a black look from her mother began relating the requested story, "It was while I was still in high school. I'd been to the basketball game with Greg Johnson. We came back here to watch the late move and listen to records."

"The weather got really bad and Dad said he didn't think Greg should try to drive back up north in the blowing snow. I got some spare blankets out of Mom's old wardrobe and Greg bedded down on the davenport in the living room, and the rest of us went to bed."

Pam paused to take a drink of ice tea before continuing with her story. "About four o'clock we heard Greg yelling bloody murder, and we all came running down to see what was going on. The yard light lit up the living room and I could see Greg sitting on the davenport just shouting his head off.

"Dad flipped on the living room light and asked him what was going on." With a teasing look at her father she added, "As I remember it, his language was a little more colorful than that!"

Everybody chuckled knowing how Paul sometimes lapsed into language that made Ellen raise her eyebrows in alarm.

Pam continued, "When Greg finally calmed down, he told us the most amazing story. He'd been sound asleep and woke up suddenly. The house was deathly silent, and the blanket that was thrown loosely over him felt like it was stretched so tightly

(144)

that he couldn't move from the neck down. It didn't exactly hurt, but he couldn't get up or anything.

"When Greg opened his eyes he saw the figure of a bearded man standing by the couch clutching a cat. It spoke to him saying in a sad voice 'It's dead. What should I do?' Then it vanished.

"Greg refused to close his eyes again that night, and he always acted funny if he had to be in the living room by himself. He certainly never stayed overnight again." Pam finished.

Her father added thoughtfully, "We asked around after that and learned that an older man was killed on the farm. I never did find out if he was a previous owner or a hired hand. It was back before they put electric ignition on tractors. He was starting one of the old hand crank Farmall A's. Somehow when it started, it ran him over and he died shortly after." He paused to flip the top and take a drink out of the can in his hand, "We never have figured out who the other one might be. It seems to be a young girl."

Ellen had had enough, "Well, are you going to stand around and talk all day or are we going to have a fish boil?"

CHAPTER XIX

THE SOLDIER

Back a few years, before the barn burned down on the old Brownlea place, an aspiring county artist had an old experience on the old farmstead out on Townline Road east of Fish Creek.

The artist had been working most of the afternoon on a painting of the big, slightly dilapidated log barn. Things had gone well, and just a few touches were required for the work to be finished. Unfortunately, those touches were in an area of the painting that was still wet and he would have to wait for the paint to dry some before the final strokes could be added.

He stood up from his easel twisting his neck and flexing his cramped shoulders to relieve the muscle tension of the last hour's concentrated work. He balanced his brush and paints on the scarred porch railing beside his easel.

Up until this time he really hadn't paid much attention to the abandoned farmhouse. All of his energy had been focused on the work developing beneath his brush.

An ancient tree shaded the porch. Its floor boards were worn smooth by the passage of countless feet and the weathering effects of wind, rain, and snow. Faint traces of brown paint remained along the wall against the house and grooves worn in the boards between the steps and the front door indicated an often trod area.

A broken wooden chair leaned crookedly against the porch railing, and a gentle breeze stirred the previous fall's leaves trapped by spider webs in the corner of the porch. Years had passed since an industrious farm woman's broom had scattered nature's clutter marking the area as inhabited. Yet, the front door stood open.

 A few inches separated the door and the frame. He pushed it shut and then giving in to curiosity turned the ornate brass handle to see if it would open. The humidity swollen door stuck in the sagging frame, but with a strong pull the artist separated the two. The piercing grate of rusty hinges caused shivers to run up his spine as he pulled the door open.

How many of us when faced with the double temptation of spare time and an unlocked, abandoned house at our finger tips would be able to resist the temptation to explore?

It was a simple matter to pull the door open far enough to step inside. Dust motes hung in the light beams cast on the flowered carpet as the late afternoon sunlight filtered through dingy windows.

Bulky old-fashioned furniture squatted ponderously on the faded carpet. The fireplace mantel on the far wall was cluttered with the treasures of daily living. Lacy hand-crocheted doilies aged yellow by time lay under the collection of bric brac and books that covered the tables. Over everything a thick layer of dust rested like a heavy blanket.

A short hallway led back to the kitchen. Just as in the living room the kitchen looked inhabited except for the thick layer of dust that lay over everything. Big gallon jars of flour and sugar stood on the open shelves beside glass quart jars of garden produce home canned many long years before and no longer even identifiable by color, everything having taken on a uniform greenish beige tinge.

Magazines and papers were stacked on the corner of the scarred wooden table and a wood box stacked with stove wood stood in the corner near the big old cook stove.

On the far wall of the kitchen a narrow door opened onto an even narrower stairway. Carefully

testing the steps for rotted boards, the artist climbed the stairs.

Two rooms opened off the tiny landing at the top
of the steps. The first contained a bed, bureau, and
small straight-
backed chair. The
second had ob-
viously been in
regular use when
the house was
abandoned. A
woman's clothes
hung on the pegs

in the open closet. Practical black hightop shoes were neatly lined up beneath them.

The tables and dressers were cluttered with the same collection of figurines and mementoes that abounded in the living room. As with the downstairs, a thick layer of dust muted the colors of all the objects.

The painter stood on the multi-colored rag rug in front of the dresser. On its top lay a silver-backed

brush with its matching comb and mirror. Ornate bottles of perfume and creams occupied a small tray, and across the back of the chest framed pictures stood in a row.

It was a collection similar to those seen on most grandmothers' bureaus. Husband, children, and grandchildren captured forever at various ages in black and white stillness.

Certainly not unusual except the trained artist's eye noted that one picture, a young man dressed in an army uniform dating back to World War I, was not shrouded with the same blanket of dust that hung on everything else in the room. It almost glowed in the fading afternoon light appearing to have been rubbed free of the invasive dust. With a last look around, the artist left the room returning to the downstairs and his waiting painting.

As he left the house, he carefully flipped the aged locking mechanism on the latch before pulling the door firmly closed against other intruders. Some wouldn't merely look. Out of idleness or greed they would vandalize or steal from the old house. He checked to make sure the catch was secure and the door definitely locked before returning to his painting.

Just as he finished his work and began packing his gear, a familiar grating screech echoed in the gathering darkness. The painter turned, climbed the steps to the house, and stood in front of the open door. How could a door that fit so tightly swing open of its own accord, especially when securely locked?

No wind stirred that might have blown it open. The blades of the rickety windmill lay idle no longer turning in the soft breeze that had spun them slowly all afternoon. Still puzzled he relocked the door, loaded his equipment into his car and left.

That night the artist woke in a cold sweat. The images that had been passing through his mind as he slept were just as vivid upon wakening. A tiny sparrow of a woman, bent and grayed by age, lovingly polished the picture of her much adored youngest attired in his neatly pressed lieutenant's uniform on the hem of her print apron. She walked down the rickety steps passing through the kitchen and sitting room to the front door.

(152)

She propped it open so Johnny could get in if he came home while she was asleep and not up to welcome him. Horace said that Johnny wouldn't come home, that the fields of France would always hold him, but Horace didn't know. Johnny would be home, home to his mama. He'd promised before he left.

The artist went back to the farm one time after that. The door to the old house was open.

Eventually the house was sold. The new owners stripped the interior of all trace of the previous inhabitants and turned it into a gift shop and gallery. Did a new lock and the removal of Johnny's picture end the woman's lonely vigil?

CHAPTER XX

THE SPECIAL GIFT

n the words of his granddaughter, "Grandpa Klaus was a see'r. He seemed to know things that the rest of us didn't. Things that you just couldn't know. Things like babies being born or a neighbor dying before his time. He never could explain how he came to know it, just said that he 'saw' it and knew it was gonna happen."

Klaus's story began a long time before he emigrated to the United States. Even as a boy in the old country he knew about his gift. It was that very gift that led him from his dearly loved homeland to Chicago and northward on the Goodrich Line's steamer *Carolina* to Sister Bay in the early 1900's.

When pressed about his reasons for leaving his native Germany, gentle Klaus would quietly reply, "Because all I can see in her future is death and destruction. If I stayed there, I would die. Germany's future is war."

As a lad in Germany, Klaus was trained as a shepherd. His eyes permanently red from long hours spent in the winds and bright sun of the hills  that surrounded his village. When he was called in for military service, he pretended to not be able to see and managed to avoid the German draft.

A short time later, Klaus fled his homeland with just what he could carry on his back, but during his lifetime he never regretted his actions.

Klaus settled a piece of ground just off Old Stage Road in the center of the peninsula. He cleared the brush, cut the trees, and planted potatoes around the stumps for food and to trade for goods at the store.

The following year he bought a few sheep, planted hay, and built a small frame house. Evidently Klaus built well because his original house still stands. It's been enlarged and remodeled over the years but its weathered wood is a graceful reminder of its age.

Before he built the granary or the barns, Klaus stored his precious crops in the upper part of the house to protect them from the weather and animals. During the last major remodeling, the workmen found grain that had filtered through the upstairs floorboards to settle on the ceiling of the room below.

Even in the new country, life wasn't easy for Klaus. He married a young widow with small children. During their time together, Klaus fathered a handsome son and baby daughter, but his lovely Katarina died shortly after the baby was born and soon the infant was gone, too.

After a few years, Klaus remarried and began a family with his young bride. She always insisted that it was his sparkling blue eyes and kind, gentle manner that she fell in love with, not the weathered face concealed beneath a neatly trimmed beard and mustache.

Klaus worked hard from sunup to sundown tending his stock and crops, cutting wood, and hunting for game for the table. His hours were full with little time left for foolish notions.

Perhaps that is why he ignored the feeling he had while crossing the bridge over the creek one October day. But the next week the feeling was still there, stronger even, and Klaus stopped to investigate.

(157)

On the near side of the bridge, he felt warmth and turning his head to the right Klaus saw a glowing image. It reached down to the brush along the creek bank. Klaus retraced his steps to that side of the bridge and slid down the rocky bank. There in the weeds at the edge of the water lay a man's body.

Of course, many of the neighbors tried to discount Klaus's gift, but even the staunchest had to admit that he had a peculiar knack for guessing right about things. Henry Miller became a believer when Klaus correctly foretold that Henry's wife Della was pregnant with a longed-for child.

When pressed to explain how he know such things, Klaus would shrug his narrow shoulders and say that sometimes he just felt it and other times he would see a sign.

To Klaus the image of a cradle up by the chimney of a house indicated an upcoming birth for the family just as the vision of a coffin meant that a death would soon occur.

Klaus foretold his own death months in advance. As he became older and was no longer able to do a full day's work, one of his sons took over the farm. Klaus lived in the house with the son, his young wife, and their school-age child.

Klaus was delighted when he 'saw' that yet another baby would be born in the family and predicted that he would hold the baby just before his own death.

As Klaus was in quite good health at the time, the daughter-in-law discounted his words as the ramblings of an active imagination.

Klaus's last wish was granted. He lived just a few days past the birth of the baby girl. He held the child in his arms and with tears blearing his faded blue eyes said, "Raise the baby good, the same way you did the other one."

That child, now a grandmother herself, finished

Klaus' story with these words, "Mama said that the day Grandpa died his old sheep dog Fritz didn't want to be outside. The minute he was put out in the yard he began howling and wouldn't quit. When they let him back in, he went immediately to Grandpa's bed and laid his nose by Grandpa's head and kept howling. Grandpa was dead."

CHAPTER XXI

THE LITTLE PEOPLE

 oung Anna was a happy but quiet child. She had few toys as was the case for most small children in the 1850's when the essentials of food, shelter and safety, not the entertainment of their children, occupied the minds and snapped the energy of parents.

The early Icelandic settlers of Washington Island faced many hardships. Their perilous ship voyage was over but few belongings made the journey with them. They were forced to rely on their own resourcefulness and the land itself for food and shelter. The isolation of the island made this even more true.

That first spring and summer Anna's father and two older brothers cleared the timber on a small rise not far from what is now kown as Jackson Harbor. They trimmed the biggest logs and notched them to erect the tiny cabin that was home that

first winter. A sleeping loft for the young ones was reached by climbing the crude ladder propped against the fireplace wall.

Anna's mormor, her mother's mother, lived with them. While Anna's mother was busy doing wash, tending the small garden, or caring for baby Hans Anna played at her Grandmother's feet.

With the steady thrum of her spinning wheel for accompaniment, Grandmother sang folk songs and told the tales handed down from generation to generation. Tales of life in an inhospitable climate, legends of the huldrefolk, little people similar to the leprechauns of Ireland, who hid in the meadows around her native village, and stories of Anna's mother's childhood were often repeated to the delight of the young Anna.

With strict warnings to stay away from the swamp

to the west, Anna was permitted to play in the meadows and woods that surrounded their tiny cabin. She seemed to have a natural affinity for the woods and wildlife and thoroughly enjoyed her quiet life.

During the summer, it was Anna's job to gather the wild berries that grew abundantly on the island. It was a chore that she enjoyed since it allowed her to play in the woods.

It was with a light heart that Anna skipped down the dusty dirt path on her way to the west meadow to pick the last of the summer's raspberries. Mama had promised to make tebrod, Anna's favorite sweet bread filled with fruit, if Anna brought her a pail of berries. Bright August sunshine glinted off Anna's blond braids as she hurried along softly humming her favorite song.

When she returned several hours later, Anna was still happily humming but the bucket she set on bucket the plank table was barely half full.

Now Anna's mother, as is the way with many mothers, took one look at a half full bucket that she very well knew should have been brimming over the top with bright red berries and immediately suspected that her daughter had done more playing than berry picking.

She questioned Anna in a sharper tone than might have been the case had she not had an unusually trying day herself, "And so, child, why is your bucket so empty? Did you fall asleep in the shade of the big tree again?"

So happy that she was unaware of her mother's anger Anna blithely answered, "Oh, no, Mama. I wanted the tebrod very badly so I wouldn't fall asleep, but they came and said they were so very hungry and would I leave the berries for them." Her blue eyes danced with barely suppressed excitement.

"Who said that?" her mother questioned sharply. "Who feels that they have more need of food than we do, that we should not have it and they should?"

"Why the huldrefolk, of course. I saw them, Mama. I saw the hidden people. They're just like they are in Mormor's stories, but much nicer." Anna excitedly continued, "They had tiny clothes, and little shoes, and funny hats. We talked and they even

(164)

let me dance with them when I said that they might have the berries. They taught me a new song it goes like this." She sang a haunting melody.

Unfortunately, for Anna her mother did not share her excitement, nor did she believe in the existence of the hidden people.

Young Anna received a severe scolding about her irresponsibility and laziness with a tart reprimand about inventing tales and letting her imagination run away with her thrown in for good measure.

Her mother left the cabin to tend to the evening chores and a tearful Anna sank to the floor beside her Grandmother's rocker. The old chair creaked to a stop as Anna's head sank to the apron-covered lap for comfort.

"I did see them, Mormor. I really did. I didn't make it up!" The old lady dried the child's eyes with the corner of her apron and smoothed the damp tendrils of blond hair back away from the tear-stained face with her arthritic fingers.

"I know, child, I know that you were telling the truth."

Lost in her own reflections, the old woman con-

tinued in a voice cracked with age, "I'd forgotten that song. So many years. Back home, back when I was a child just your age, my grandmother, used to sing it to me. She'd sing the song and then tell me of the time that she, like you, found the huldrefolk and spent the day with them, and how they danced and taught her the words and melody to that special song."

EPILOGUE

So, do "the hidden people" with their tiny shoes and funny hats still frolic in the meadows of Washington Island? And, what in the world was going on with that tiny bird that guided Judd and Hermie home, and in such heavy snow, yet? Does Grandpa Wetterstra still stop by to catch up on the news, or does Louise still visit with friends in that little apartment above the store? Some of these things, I guess, we'll never know.

INDEX
(Chapter Titles are in Capital Letters)

INDEX

(173)

(174)

If you have enjoyed this book, perhaps you would enjoy others from Quixote Press.

GHOSTS OF THE MISSISSIPPI RIVER
Mpls. to Dubuque by Bruce Carlson ...... paperback **$9.95**

GHOSTS OF THE MISSISSIPPI RIVER
Dubuque to Keokuk by Bruce Carlson ..... paperback **$9.95**

GHOSTS OF THE MISSISSIPPI RIVER
Keokuk to St. Louis by Bruce Carlson ..... paperback **$9.95**

HOW TO TALK MIDWESTERN
by Robert Thomas .... paperback **$7.95**

GHOSTS OF SCOTT COUNTY, IOWA
by Bruce Carlson .... hardback **$12.95**

GHOSTS OF ROCK ISLAND COUNTY, ILLINOIS
by Bruce Carlson .... hardback **$12.95**

GHOSTS OF THE AMANA COLONIES
by Lori Erickson .... paperback **$9.95**

GHOSTS OF NORTHEAST IOWA
by Ruth Hein and Vicky Hinsenbrock ..... paperback **$9.95**

GHOSTS OF POLK COUNTY, IOWA
by Tom Welch .... paperback **$9.95**

GHOSTS OF THE IOWA GREAT LAKES
by Bruce Carlson .... paperback **$9.95**

MEMOIRS OF A DAKOTA HUNTER
by Gary Scholl .... paperback **$9.95**

LOST AND BURIED TREASURE ALONG THE MISSISSIPPI
by Gary Scholl and Netha Bell .... paperback **$7.95**

MISSISSIPPI RIVER PO' FOLK
by Pat Wallace .... paperback **$9.95**

(177)

STRANGE FOLKS ALONG THE MISSISSIPPI
by Pat Wallace ....paperback $9.95

THE VANISHING OUTHOUSE OF IOWA
by Bruce Carlson ....paperback $9.95

THE VANISHING OUTHOUSE OF ILLINOIS
by Bruce Carlson ....paperback $9.95

THE VANISHING OUTHOUSE OF MINNESOTA
by Bruce Carlson ....paperback $9.95

THE VANISHING OUTHOUSE OF WISCONSIN
by Bruce Carlson ....paperback $9.95

MISSISSIPPI RIVER COOKIN' BOOK
by Bruce Carlson ....paperback $11.95

IOWA'S ROAD KILL COOKBOOK
by Bruce Carlson ....paperback $7.95

HITCH HIKING THE UPPER MIDWEST
by Bruce Carlson ....paperback $7.95

IOWA, THE LAND BETWEEN THE VOWELS
by Bruce Carlson ....paperback $9.95
(Farm Boy Stories From the Early 1900's)

GHOSTS OF SOUTHWEST MINNESOTA
by Ruth Hein.........................paperback $9.95

ME 'N WESLEY
by Bruce Carlson ....paperback $9.95
(Stories about the homemade toys that farm children made and played with around the turn of the century.)

SOUTH DAKOTA ROAD KILL COOKBOOK
by Bruce Carlson ....paperback $7.95

GHOSTS OF THE BLACK HILLS
by Tom Welch.........................paperback $9.95

Some Pretty Tame, But Kinda Funny Stories About Early DAKOTA LADIES-OF-THE-EVENING
by Bruce Carlson ....paperback $9.95

**Some Pretty Tame, But Kinda Funny Stories
About Early IOWA LADIES-OF-THE EVENING**
by Bruce Carlson .... paperback $9.95

**Some Pretty Tame, But Kinda Funny Stories
About Early ILLINOIS LADIES-OF-THE-EVENING**
by Bruce Carlson .... paperback $9.95

**Some Pretty Tame, But Kinda Funny Stories
About Early MINNESOTA
LADIES-OF-THE-EVENING**
by Bruce Carlson .... paperback $9.95

**Some Pretty Tame, But Kinda Funny Stories
About Early WISCONSIN
LADIES-OF-THE-EVENING**
by Bruce Carlson .... paperback $9.95

**Some Pretty Tame, But Kinda Funny Stories
About Early MISSOURI LADIES-OF-THE-EVENING**
by Bruce Carlson .... paperback $9.95

THE DAKOTA'S VANISHING OUTHOUSE
Bruce Carlson .... paperback $9.95

ILLINOIS' ROAD KILL COOKBOOK
by Bruce Carlson .... paperback $7.95

OLD IOWA HOUSES, YOUNG LOVES
by Bruce Carlson .... paperback $9.95
(Stores about old houses in Iowa and young loves they have known.)

TERROR IN THE BLACK HILLS
Dick Kennedy .... paperback $9.95

IOWA'S EARLY HOME REMEDIES
by various .... paperback $9.95

THE VANISHING OUTHOUSE OF MISSOURI
by Bruce Carlson .... paperback $9.95

JACK KING VS. DETECTIVE MacKENZIE
by N. Bell............................ paperback $9.95

RIVER SHARKS & SHENANIGANS
(Tales of Riverboat Gambling of Years Ago)
by N. Bell...........................paperback $9.95

TALES OF HACKETT'S CREEK
(1940's Mississippi River Kids)
by D. Titus..........................paperback $9.95

LOST & BURIED TREASURE OF THE
MISSOURI RIVER
by N. Bell...........................paperback $9.95

GHOSTS OF THE OZARKS
by Bruce Carlson ....paperback $9.95

UNSOLVED MYSTERIES OF THE MISSISSIPPI
by N. Bell...........................paperback $9.95

TALL TALES OF THE MISSISSIPPI RIVER
by D. Titus..........................paperback $9.95

TALL TALES OF THE MISSOURI RIVER
by D. Titus..........................paperback $9.95

MAKIN' DO IN SOUTH DAKOTA
by various ....paperback $9.95

TRICKS WE PLAYED IN IOWA
by various ....paperback $9.95

CHILDREN OF THE RIVER
by various ....paperback $9.95

LET'S GO DOWN TO THE RIVER 'AN . . .
by various ....paperback $9.95

EARLY WISCONSIN HOME REMEDIES
by various ....paperback $9.95

EARLY MISSOURI HOME REMEDIES
by various ....paperback $9.95

MY VERY FIRST . . .
by various ....paperback $9.95

101 WAYS FOR IOWANS TO "DO IN THEIR NEIGHBOR'S PESKY DOG WITHOUT GETTING CAUGHT

by Bruce Carlson .... paperback $7.95

SOUTH DAKOTA ROADKILL COOKBOOK

by Bruce Carlson .... paperback $9.95

A FIELD GUIDE TO IOWA'S CRITTERS

by Bruce Carlson .... paperback $7.95

A FIELD GUIDE TO MISSOURI'S CRITTERS

by Bruce Carlson .... paperback $7.95

MISSOURI'S ROADKILL COOKBOOK

by Bruce Carlson .... paperback $7.95

A FIELD GUIDE TO ILLINOIS' CRITTERS

by Bruce Carlson .... paperback $7.95

MINNESOTA'S ROADKILL COOKBOOK

by Bruce Carlson .... paperback $7.95

REVENGE OF THE ROADKILL

by Bruce Carlson .... paperback $7.95

THE MOTORIST'S FIELD GUIDE TO MIDWEST FARM EQUIPMENT

(Misguided Information as only a City Slicker can get it messed up.)
by Bruce Carlson .... paperback $7.95

ILLINOIS EARLY HOME REMEDIES

by various .... paperback $9.95

GUNSHOOTIN', WHISKEY DRINKIN', GIRL CHASIN' TALES OUT OF THE OLD DAKOTA TERRITORY

by Netha Bell .... paperback $9.95

EARLY IOWA SCHOOLS

by C. Johnston .... paperback $9.95

WYOMING'S ROADKILL COOKBOOK

by Bruce Carlson .... paperback $7.95

(181)

MONTANA'S ROADKILL COOKBOOK
by B. Carlson . . . . paperback $7.95

DOWNHOME IN NEBRASKA
(Tales of Nebraska Housewife)
by M. Walsh . . . . paperback $9.95

SKUNK RIVER ANTHOLOGY
by Gene "Will" Olson . . . . paperback $9.95

FUNNER-THINGS-TO-DO-THAN-COOKIN'
COOKBOOK
by Louise Lum . . . . paperback $11.95

101 WAYS TO USE A DEAD RIVER FLY
by Bruce Carlson . . . . paperback $7.95

MAKIN' DO IN ILLINOIS
by various authors . . . . paperback $9.95

MISSOURI'S OLD HOUSES, AND NEW LOVES
by Bruce Carlson . . . . paperback $9.95

YOU KNOW YOU'RE IN IOWA WHEN . . .
by Bruce Carlson . . . . paperback $7.95

IOWA - A JOURNEY IN A PROMISED LAND
by Kathy Yoder . . . . paperback $16.95

WISCONSIN'S ROADKILL COOKBOOK
by Bruce Carlson . . . . paperback $7.95

UNDERGROUND MISSOURI
by Bruce Carlson . . . . paperback $9.95

GUNSHOOTIN', WHISKEY DRINKIN', GIRL
CHASIN' STORIES OUT OF THE OLD
MISSOURI TERRITORY
by Bruce Carlson . . . . paperback $9.95

VACANT LOT, SCHOOL YARD & BACK ALLEY GAMES OF THE MIDWEST YEARS AGO

by various authors .... paperback $9.95

HOW SOME OF US ITTY-BITTY FOLKS HERE IN THE MIDWEST WOULD RUN A HOUSE IF WE HAD TO

by various authors .... paperback $7.95

GUNSHOOTIN', WHISKEY DRINKIN', GIRL CHASIN' STORIES OUT OF THE LAND OF THE LAKES

by Netha Bell .... paperback $9.95

Need A Gift?

For

- Shower • Birthday • Mother's Day •
- Anniversary • Christmas •

Turn Page for Order Form
(Order Now While Supply Lasts!)

To Order Copies Of

Ghosts of Door County, Wisconsin

Please send me _____ copies of **Ghosts of Door County, Wisconsin** at $9.95 each. (Make checks payable to **QUIXOTE PRESS.**)

Name _____

Street _____

City _____ State _____ Zip _____

Send Orders To:

Quixote Press
3544 Blakslee St.
Wever, IA 52658

- -

To Order Copies Of

Ghosts of Door County, Wisconsin

Please send me _____ copies of **Ghosts of Door County, Wisconsin** at $9.95 each. (Make checks payable to **QUIXOTE PRESS.**)

Name _____

Street _____

City _____ State _____ Zip _____

Send Orders To:
Quixote Press
3544 Blakslee St.
Wever, IA 52658